PRAISE FOR

MAKE LIFE BEAUTIFUL

"*Make Life Beautiful* is a necessary reminder that there is inherent beauty and warmth in all moments. Shea and Syd invite us into endearing conversations filled with wit, humor, and creativity, and an honesty shining a light on the couple's beautiful focal points."

—ALYSSA ROSENHECK, INTERIORS AND ARCHITECTURAL PHOTOGRAPHER,
STYLIST, AND AUTHOR OF *THE NEW SOUTHERN STYLE*

"*Make Life Beautiful* is raw, honest, and motivating. A captivating read as Shea and Syd navigate us through the early days of their relationship, family, and business. A form of a modern-day romance success story. I enjoyed reading about their compelling journey, which shaped the design empire we know as Studio McGee. Truly inspiring in every way."

—MONIKA HIBBS, FOUNDER AND CREATIVE DIRECTOR OF
MONIKA HIBBS AND AUTHOR OF *GATHER AT HOME*

"In a world of picture perfect, Syd and Shea are a much-needed breath of fresh air. It takes courage to admit that things aren't always perfect. I applaud them for authentically sharing their story with the world."

—MIKEL WELCH, INTERIOR DESIGNER, LIFESTYLE EXPERT,
AND TV HOST OF *MURDER HOUSE FLIP*

"There's nothing more beautiful than taking a leap and devoting your life and your heart and your work to helping other people enjoy beauty in their own homes. We've all come to know, love, and yearn for the Studio McGee look, but hearing the humble 'hows' behind the empire is even more moving and motivating. This isn't about just making your home beautiful—this is about making your *life* beautiful. Shea and Syd are talented (obviously) but they're also dreamers and supporters and risk-takers and pioneers and, somehow, still completely down-to-earth. My heart is warm, and I'm now taking notes on more than mixing patterns."

—JULIA MARCUM, COFOUNDER OF CHRIS LOVES JULIA,
GOOD INFLUENCE(R), AND PROPERTEE

MAKE LIFE
BEAUTIFUL

MAKE LIFE BEAUTIFUL

———

SYD AND SHEA McGEE

HARPER HORIZON

Published by Harper Horizon, an imprint of HarperCollins Focus LLC.

Any internet addresses, phone numbers, or company or product information printed in this book are offered as a resource and are not intended in any way to be or to imply an endorsement by Harper Horizon, nor does Harper Horizon vouch for the existence, content, or services of these sites, phone numbers, companies, or products beyond the life of this book.

ISBN 978-0-7852-3388-6 (eBook)
ISBN 978-0-7852-3387-9 (HC)
ISBN 978-1-4041-1488-3 (custom)

Library of Congress Cataloging-in-Publication Data
Library of Congress Control Number: 2020938622

Printed in the United States of America
20 21 22 23 LSC 10 9 8 7 6 5 4 3 2 1

To our parents, who never once questioned our decision to forge a new path for our lives. And to our children, Wren and Ivy, may you always see your own natural light.

CONTENTS

one

CREATE A FOCAL POINT

| *Visualize the outcome when*
| *designing your home and life.*

Shea

It all started with a set of bookshelves.

They were twelve feet high by fifteen feet wide, freshly lacquered in crisp white paint, and placed behind a black baby grand piano in a new multimillion-dollar estate. The home was in a gated neighborhood in Orange County, California, situated at the top of a hill with views of the Pacific Ocean. I stood in the formal living room, with shopping bags at my feet, and took a deep breath before climbing the ladder to clear the shelves of the piles of books and mementos so I could see the potential in front of me. I started with the lowest shelves and worked my way up the ladder one step at a time. Removing clutter applied to more than my clients' library; it was an exercise in purging the collection of doubts distracting me from what I wanted to become. What had started as an interest in design became a hobby that turned into a dream to own a business, but I didn't feel qualified to make the reach.

Before the bookshelves there was "consulting." And by consulting, I mean I would go to friends' homes and suggest pillows or help rearrange their furniture for free. When neighbors saw us unloading furniture from Syd's truck, they'd peek their heads into our windows to see the latest design project my husband, Syd, and I were tackling. Often I'd receive a text from friends, with pictures, asking for my opinion. "We're stuck on what to do with this blank wall. Do you have any ideas?" I was honored to share my thoughts and would respond with links to artwork or mirrors. "You need a large focal point to center the wall," I'd say. "Start there, and then you can add a console with a lamp, and I think you may even have room for a tree."

It was no secret that I loved design. I was taking classes at a local community college and would regularly share photos of our house projects with friends and family as we bounced from rental to rental and eventually settled into our first home. What they didn't know was that I yearned to turn my hobby into something more. Not one to make hasty decisions, I had begun piecing together a strategy to start an interior design business. I worked as a contract employee writing content for an advertising firm while taking design classes and had lost all interest in marketing for other companies. When developing web copy or blog posts, my mind would drift to planning the marketing strategy for launching my own design business. We wanted to start having kids soon, and I was enticed by the flexibility of being my own boss. The days of cold calls and sales pitches were gone. I knew I needed to start small, be patient, and let the business grow organically. If my work had merit, I was certain sharing pictures of our home on Instagram and free consulting for neighbors would pay off.

Syd understood me. He has always been my clear-sighted confidant, gently pushing me to fearlessly pursue my obvious dream. He was the one who nudged me along and kept telling me to go for it, even when I felt like a fraud. The one who encouraged me to strike a deal to trade design advice for a set of business cards in case they came in handy one day. The one who told me to take a few night classes even though I had graduated with a communications degree only a few years prior.

I had stacks of magazines with dog-eared corners and sticky notes, but zero professional experience in the field—no internships, retail experience, or even a rich auntie who had let me design her vacation home. A love for the subject hardly qualified me to charge money. However, when my sister-in-law texted me and asked me if I'd be interested in styling a giant set of built-ins for her friend, I didn't hesitate. "Yes, I can do that," I replied as though I'd been doing this work my entire life.

Then she asked how much I would charge. I immediately turned to Syd. "How much should I charge?" With that came an immediate rush of panic and excitement. I had learned in school that the going rate for interior design services was $150 an hour, and since I felt like I was half a designer, I settled on $75 an hour.

Syd

Shea said she felt half-qualified to do the job, but her thought process was much more strategic than she let on. Since she had barely started taking design classes, these bookshelves gave her a chance to learn on the job, which was more than school could offer her. Even though this project was small, it also gave her a chance to start building her portfolio, which would lead to even more work. And since she was charging half the going rate, more people would be willing to take a chance and hire her. Though Shea battled feeling like an impostor, she always had a plan.

I knew Shea could do this. Not just the bookshelves, but all of it—everything that has become Studio McGee. She has always been creative but was too logical to accept her talent could lead to a career. Shea infuses beauty into everything she touches. From dinners on the patio to decorating around a hand-me-down IKEA couch, I've seen her turn the most mundane moments into masterpieces. Whether it's a one-bedroom apartment or a million-dollar house, she has the ability to make people feel something when they are immersed in surroundings she's designed. It's not about glitz—it's about creating an environment that balances beauty and comfort. I've been lucky to be a beneficiary of those surroundings and wanted other people to experience that too.

But with only a few classes under her belt, Shea struggled with viewing herself as a *professional* designer without a degree or certification. We spent many nights discussing this mental roadblock, long before the bookshelves came along. She has impeccable taste and style, and to me, she seemed like a natural. She spent so much time reading design blogs, books, and magazines, that was all she wanted to talk about. She wanted to launch a design business more than anything, but Shea's a planner and likes to play by the rules. It was hard for her to make the leap from passion to career path. In her mind, you had to follow certain steps before you could officially start a career. I, on the other hand, believe you learn by doing. I kept telling her to jump in and go for it.

Shea didn't exactly jump in. I'd say it was more like wading slowly until she found herself staring at those bookshelves. But once the opportunity was in front of her, she knew this was the chance she'd been waiting for.

Shea

When I went over to my client's house for our first meeting, I was twenty-six and wanted to come across like I knew what I was doing. I was all business. With time, I've learned to relax and be myself. I've learned your expertise will reveal itself in the work, but connection is equally important. But on that first job I was anxious and got straight to the point: "Hi. How are you? Let's have a look at those built-ins."

I asked about her personal style. She told me that although the exterior of her home was a Tuscan style, she liked modern design with a lot of white, gray, and light wood tones. She said, "My husband has hundreds of books, and they just look like a mess on these shelves. This wall is the first thing you see when you walk into our house, and I want it to make a statement."

She took me on a brief tour of her home, and I paid close attention to how she'd decorated the rest of her house to see what she was naturally drawn to. Selections made by a homeowner without the assistance of an interior designer are cues to me about what is comfortable for the client. I create with their natural tendencies in mind and also consider where to try new things. I made some notes, took measurements, and snapped a few pictures. The floors throughout the main level were a warm travertine paired with light-gray walls. Each room was spacious, with tall ceilings and French doors that opened to various courtyards. The furniture was a mix of old pieces that were lacquered the same white as the built-ins and new pieces with more of a contemporary, Hollywood Regency style. As I visualized the outcome of the built-ins, I knew that adding natural textures to the shelves would help soften the hard edges and create a more inviting atmosphere upon entering their home.

We set up a time for me to return to complete the project, and she asked how much I thought it would cost to decorate the built-ins. I'd already spent hours online scoping out boxes and frames and vases and anything else I might need to fill this space, so I guessed a dollar amount. It turned out I used every single item I purchased, and that my guess was quite accurate. (I later learned it's better to plan for more than you need.)

That day I was nervous, and I tried to leave before she could ask me any questions about my qualifications. In hindsight, it's hilarious I thought anyone would ask me about my degree to place a few objects on bookshelves, but I'd replayed that scenario in my head every day leading up to our meeting and had convinced myself she was going to question my credentials.

For half a day I ran around to different stores, buying what I needed, and then spent weeks mulling over how I'd pull everything together. I'd make little sketches and fall asleep rearranging those built-ins in my mind like a game of Tetris.

I drove over to my client's house on a midsummer Saturday. My car was loaded with everything I thought I was going to need. She let me know she was going to be in and out all day because she had a lot of errands to run. I was glad. Even though I felt prepared, the last thing I wanted on this first job was the pressure of someone watching over my shoulder.

After she left, I spent the day running up and down a ladder, arranging and rearranging each vignette. In the design world we use the word *vignette* to refer to a small yet pleasing view. I like to ask myself, *If I were to take a picture of this moment, is the composition strong enough to stand alone?* A beautiful room is composed of small vignettes working in harmony. The built-ins contained closed cabinetry across the bottom and a grid of thirty open cubbies above. The goal was to create a well-balanced focal wall with all of the shelves working in sync, but with each shelf able to stand alone as its own vignette.

My clients' collection included books, manuals, sheet music, photos, and plaques. All of these shapes were rectangular and fell flat when styled alone. To add texture I sprinkled materials like pieces of driftwood, rocks, coral, and moss throughout the shelves to bring an organic quality to a very linear wall. Between the books and boxes, I placed a glass dome over a piece of coral, a dusty, green succulent next to a family picture, and a geode cracked open to reveal cream-colored crystals.

If I grouped three items on one shelf, I'd place one large vase above it to give the eye a moment to rest. The balance of busy and calm throughout the design allowed the viewer to appreciate the whole wall instead of being distracted by too many items. I paid attention to levels, shape, and materiality by playing with different ways to stack books and utilize objects as bookends. I brought lidded seagrass baskets to hide the sheet music and a few potted plants to add natural greenery. The palette was primarily black, white, and neutral, with hints of color from the book spines.

I'd place everything and stand back with my arms folded and head tilted to one side, looking everything over. Then I'd run back up the ladder and move more things around. I must have rearranged all the big pieces fifty times. I said a lot of silent prayers as I climbed that ladder.

The more you design, the easier and more natural it becomes. It wasn't easy or natural on that day, and I was sweating every detail. The journey to the end result was more laborious than I'd anticipated, and I lacked the confidence to appreciate the art of refinement. Early in my career I saw changes in my plans as an indication of my lack of competency as a designer. Over the years, though, I've realized that establishing a focal point by visualizing the outcome is an exercise in beginning. Drawing, dreaming, and planning give us direction, but flexibility often results in an outcome better than I originally envisioned. Good designs are planned, but memorable designs evolve and take shape through careful adjustments along the way. When designing your home and life, the first step is not about finding perfection from the outset—it is about doing.

Syd

The day Shea went to style the bookshelves, I headed to the ocean to surf. When I returned she was still working. I texted her a few times to check in and see how everything was coming along. She didn't respond, so I knew she was stressed. Shea never told me she was nervous, but I knew how much this first client meant to her and how much time she had spent preparing for that day. Her client lived a few blocks away from us, so I made a Diet Coke run (the first of many through the years) and surprised her. As I pulled up, she came out to the car to grab her drink through the passenger window. She grinned and said some caffeine was just what she needed, then turned to head back inside. "Wait? Aren't you going to show me how it looks in there?"

I followed her into the front room of the house and saw the floor covered in shopping bags, crumpled tissue paper, and piles of books. But when I looked up I could see she was working her magic. I thought the styling looked wonderful, but the expression on her face told me she wasn't so sure. "You're doing great," I told her. It was fun to see her taking the first step toward pursuing her dream, and I was proud. I only stayed about five minutes because I wanted to give Shea space to create. "You've got this. Relax and just do your thing," I said as I walked out the door. "This is what you've always wanted to do." Shea smiled and kept running up and down the ladder.

Shea

Syd's drive-by visit was more than Diet Coke to me—his support filled in the spaces where I lacked confidence. I stopped rearranging every item on the bookshelves and started committing to my decisions. When I finally had everything exactly the way I wanted it, I took a few pictures. My client came home and was stunned. "I can't believe it," she said. "It's beautiful!" I thanked her again, doing my best to project a professional image, but inside I was bursting with joy. I liked what I had done, but making a client happy was an added bonus I'd never experienced. I only charged her for three hours of work, the amount of time I was there styling the shelves. I didn't charge her for my time shopping, even though I should have. Did I undervalue my time? Yes. Would that be the last time? Definitely not.

When I got home, I couldn't wait to post the pictures of the built-ins on my personal Instagram, to all three hundred of my followers. People went crazy over those bookshelves. The comments ranged from "Wow! Want to come to my house?" to "Belongs in a magazine!" Even if most of the messages were from family and friends, I was encouraged. It was the first time I'd shared a design that wasn't from my own home, and I felt validated in my belief that I could turn my passion into a career. With one photo, my crazy dream of becoming a professional interior designer didn't seem so crazy anymore.

I began to establish a focal point for what a career in design would look like. With the idea of starting our family on the horizon, my dream was to work from home, establish a reputation for designs with laid-back sophistication, and become so successful that I could hire an assistant. Saying yes to my first client before finishing design school set me on that path. I was on my way to creating a life in pursuit of my passion.

Within two weeks I had another client. I didn't have a website or a portfolio yet, but I set up an Instagram account for my new business, Shea McGee Design. The platform was simple to use, and I envisioned it as a free tool to share my work and be discovered by potential clients. My first follower was my mom, and I figured that if friends and family liked my photos, people they knew could discover me, and I could grow from there. At the time I was focused on building my business and had no idea how far this Instagram journey would take me.

But long before climbing a ladder to design bookshelves, Syd and I were designing our life together.

two

MIXING STYLES

*A room speaks to the heart when you create
pairings with juxtaposition and balance.*

Shea

Finals had ended, and it was officially summer. I was heading into my junior year at Brigham Young University in Provo, Utah, far away from my childhood home in Texas. Provo is a small college town about an hour south of Salt Lake City and a twenty-minute drive from Sundance ski resort. The university is nestled at the base of the Rocky Mountains, and a large *Y* made of white stones overlooks the campus. The town is centered around Jesus, football, and gettin' married.

My parents had met there twenty years prior, and I spent my childhood wearing cougar blue sweatshirts, excited to follow in their footsteps. My younger brother, Austin, was also attending the university and had plans to move out of the dorms and into his own apartment. My large, creaky SUV, lovingly nicknamed the Ford *Exploder*, was needed to help him haul his stuff. It was white with a turquoise-green pinstripe on the side and groaned the second I tapped on the brakes. The AC was touch and go, but it had a seven-disc player, and I kept a case filled with CDs on my visor.

Austin had called me a few hours earlier to ask for a hand. On the phone he said, "My buddy Syd will be there and you're going to like him, but don't, because he's my friend." As I pulled into the lot, I knew I was in trouble. There Syd was, on a skateboard, wearing the skinniest skinny jeans I had ever seen. We went on our first date the next night.

Syd

I joined an intramural soccer team in college because I loved the game, but I'd never really played. That's where I met my future brother-in-law, Austin. He needed help moving into a new apartment and bribed me with some vending machine snacks. Not that I needed a bribe to help a friend, but it did sweeten the deal. I had no idea the perks wouldn't stop there. Enter how I met *the* Shea Miller.

I started skating as I waited for Austin's sister to show up with the car. I heard the thing before I could see it, and when Shea pulled into the lot, I turned to Austin and said, "Dang, dude. Your sister is pretty cute." He rolled his eyes and didn't say anything.

We started loading the car, and I noticed a Cat Power CD on her visor. I told her she had good taste in music for a Texan (classic flirt move: an underhanded compliment). She laughed, and we couldn't stop talking the rest of the move. I used my skateboard as a dolly, wheeling boxes from the trunk to Austin's new apartment. It was new to him, but Austin's bachelor pad had seen better days.

After we finished unloading, Shea and I sat on Austin's saggy plaid couch and chatted in the living room while he stuffed concert tees into dresser drawers. We talked about what we missed about home. Shea was from Texas and I'm from California, and we both missed the Mexican food. We discovered we were both studying communications; Shea was in the public relations program, and I was studying marketing at a nearby university.

Our conversation was interrupted when their mom came over to help Austin unpack, and we made introductions. As I was leaving, I shamelessly asked for Shea's number in front of her mom *and* brother. Shea's mom raised her eyebrow and attempted to conceal her laughter as she waited to see how Shea would react. I think Shea might have been too embarrassed to say no in front of a crowd, but hey, I took what I could get.

Shea

I was both excited and mortified. Syd never follows the rules, and I follow *all* of them. We're natural opposites, but our juxtaposition provides balance and makes life together more enjoyable.

Syd

The next night I took Shea to dinner, and we have either been together or spoken on the phone every day since.

Shea

I grew up in Houston, Texas. In high school, I drove a Jeep with a lift kit and was captain of the drill team. All of the guys I dated said "y'all" instead of "dude," and you'd better believe that *none* of them rode skateboards. Dating a surfer boy from Southern California (he always says the entire thing—not SoCal or Cali, because he claims those nicknames are a dead giveaway you're not a local) was fun and very different from any of my other relationships.

The more I learned about Syd, the more I understood what it meant to be a true "dude." Syd used words like *bro* and *gnarly*, but he was the hardest-working beach bum around. When he was just fourteen, he started "working" in a surf shop for store credit because he was too young for a real paycheck. He owned a small clothing line in high school and sold T-shirts he designed at local shops on the main street in downtown Huntington Beach. Over the summers, when he wasn't working he was at the beach. His mom would drop him off to surf all day and pick him up as the sun went down. Syd had a way of flying by the seat of his pants and making life look easy.

Unlike me.

I am a planner, and I grew up in a family of planners. My dad was an FBI agent, and my mom stayed at home to dote on my brother and me. While Dad was leading covert missions all over the world, she was a world-class stay-at-home mom. She made our lunches, drove us to lessons, and sewed every one of our Halloween costumes. When we were in high school, she styled displays for boutiques that sold candles, big Texas jewelry, and stationery. Very little was done without actionable goals and a lot of supervision in the Miller household.

My plan when I graduated from high school was set: I'd go to my parents' alma mater, graduate in four years, get a good job, work a few years, fall in love, get married, and start a family. It was all traditional and predictable, without much, if any, room for spontaneity. I found comfort in sticking with a plan, so I rarely asked questions and spent most of my time figuring out how to check items off my to-do list.

But then I met Syd.

Syd

I grew up the youngest of six kids. My family lived with a certain level of constant chaos. I have two brothers and three sisters— between me and my oldest brother, there's a fifteen-year gap. My two brothers raced BMX bikes, and I have a lot of memories of them putting me on something with wheels and then making me jump off a ramp or pulling me behind a bike or car. School was never a top priority for me, and as the youngest in the family it was easy to get away with skipping school when the surf was good. I skated by (both literally and figuratively) and finished high school with the intent to at least give college a try.

After a brief stint at Orange Coast Community College, where I took a few general courses, I left on a two-year service mission to Louisville, Kentucky, for our church. We lived in rural areas, going door-to-door sharing our gospel message and volunteering our time to help struggling farmers. We cleaned chicken coops, harvested hay, and ate the roadkill people served us. When my time in Kentucky ended, I followed a few friends to Utah and enrolled at Utah Valley University to study marketing.

Shea

Syd and I are opposites in our approach to life, but the counter-balance has always worked for us. Even dating was easy.

The only fight we ever had was about four months into our relationship, when I got a haircut. My hair was at my waist by the time I was two, and I'd kept it long enough to tie into a ponytail ever since. I had an appointment for a trim with my hairdresser, Patrick, who worked at a hipster salon in a basement south of campus. Syd's spontaneity was starting to rub off on me, and I decided it was time for a change. For the first time ever, I was going to cut off my long hair. I thought Syd would admire an impulsive decision to chop my hair into an A-line bob that brushed the top of my shoulders. When my hair was dry and I spun around to face the mirror, I felt like a new person.

I drove home to meet Syd at my apartment, and the entire time I kept glancing in the rearview mirror to admire my new haircut. I walked in the door, and Syd's reaction was a long pause, followed by, "It's all right."

"It's *all right*?" I said. Not the words any girl wants to hear about her new hairstyle. I cried.

Syd felt so bad. He kept saying, "Shea, I don't want you to cry. Shea, I feel so bad. Oh, Shea, stop crying. You know that I love you."

I stopped crying instantly. "You love me?" I said.

"Yeah," Syd said. "I love you."

He'd never said that before. All of the sadness over his reaction to my haircut disappeared. He loved me. And I loved him too. I loved Syd's free spirit, and it never occurred to me that my predictable nature was actually a trait he liked about me.

Summer came. I only had one semester left before graduating with a degree in communications and took a summer internship in California to complete the degree requirements. I had always loved design, but when I called my mom my freshman year, to tell her I was thinking of signing up for an interior design class, her response was, "But you can't draw! How are you going to do that?" It never occurred to me that I could surprise myself by learning how to draw. I didn't consider the opportunity I might miss by not even trying. I cared more about my pride than realizing a passion. Afraid to fail, I didn't take the class. I settled on a safer career path after taking an intro to PR class and saw that it could be a broadly applied major.

Syd had plans to go to Colorado for the summer with a job selling alarm systems. Neither of us really felt like the long-distance thing was going to work, and we both decided it was best if we took a break for a few months.

Syd

Shea had commitment issues when it came to us. She had reservations about how our opposite approaches to life would work together in the long term. Unlike Shea, I didn't have clear-cut plans for my future and just wanted to have a good time. I loved her, and for me, that was enough to assume we could make it work. But when she shared her hesitations about our future together, I realized I wasn't ready to get serious and agreed we both needed time apart.

Shea

I spent the summer missing Syd, and we called each other every day. I returned back to Utah from my internship in California and started my last semester. Every time he had the chance, Syd would road-trip from Denver and the two of us would hang out. We were together. And then we weren't. And then we were. And then we weren't. I struggled to understand how our contrasts as people would work well together in a long-term relationship, even though I wanted it to work out between us. We'd be happy together and then logic would take over, and I would get scared he wasn't *the one* because we weren't a perfect fit on paper.

Syd

I'd load up on Red Bulls, drive through the night, hang out with Shea for a day or two, then drive back to Colorado and go back to work all week. I just couldn't shake her.

After selling alarms all summer, I still couldn't afford college. Regardless of my finances, I was disinterested in school and wanted a break, so I moved back home to California to figure out what I was going to do next. I watched a lot of my older friends get out of school and struggle to use their degrees, so I was scared to take out loans to finish school. Plus, I was not a strong believer that you needed a college degree to be successful. My oldest brother was starting a digital marketing agency with a business partner, and he told me I could be the first employee. I took the job. He also said the opportunity could lead to something much bigger. It did.

In the meantime, Shea and I both dated other people, but I missed her. All the back and forth was driving me crazy. I knew I loved her, but I didn't understand why she couldn't make up her mind about me. I couldn't keep doing this.

Shea

I loved Syd and felt that we needed to allow ourselves the space to move on. His lack of interest in school and casual approach to everything in life terrified the planner in me. He was my best friend, and his zeal for life was contagious. Every moment with Syd was a good time, but that was also what scared me. I couldn't overcome my perception of him as the fun guy you don't get serious about. I questioned if he would be able to focus on family and career when the time came. I didn't yet see that I was too focused, and his laid-back nature was the balance I needed.

I graduated from college and took a job at a PR firm in Salt Lake City. I liked living in Utah, and my parents talked about eventually moving there. Like I said, I had a plan for my life, and I needed to get on with it. Syd and I still talked, and when he drove up to see me, I knew I loved him. But when he went back home, all my fears would come back and I'd break it off again.

My perception of Syd started to change after he went to work with his brother. He didn't just work with his brother. He worked eighteen-hour days and was laser focused on building the company. Syd's visits became fewer and further between because of his job. That's when it dawned on me that Syd may not have been interested in school, but he was always a hard worker.

My perspective of the stories he told me about working at a

a surf shop started to shift. Before, they'd made him sound like someone who loved surfing so much he'd do whatever it took to do more of it. Now it hit me: Syd had been working since he was fourteen. He loved adventure, but he also was a hard worker.

However, by this time I had a new boyfriend, and I wanted to give that relationship time to develop, even though I knew he wasn't the best guy for me and he didn't treat me the way Syd always did. Syd and I still talked on the phone (which should have been the first clue to break up with my boyfriend), and we chatted about our new jobs, what we ate for lunch, and how the surf was that day. We talked like old friends catching up on each other's lives, yet there was always an underlying sting of regret that we weren't together. But Syd was seven hundred miles away. My job was in Salt Lake City. I didn't see how we were going to change that anytime soon.

Syd

Several times I asked Shea why she was dating a tool, but she kept going out with him. Yet we kept in touch, so I knew there was still a chance. When we talked, we both knew that no other relationship lived up to the one we shared.

When we first broke up, a part of me was relieved because I wasn't ready to get serious. But after spending months apart, I knew I couldn't live without her. It was time to settle it all, and I made up my mind that if she told me there wasn't a future, that would be the end.

I drove up and laid it all out. She told me it wasn't the right time.

"Okay, if that's how you want it," I said to her. I told her I loved her but at some point, enough is enough. And in my mind, this was enough. There was no going back. "Great. Fine. We're done," I said. "I'm going back to California."

I got in my car and started back home. I had about twelve hours alone in my car to think about what had happened. My phone started ringing a couple of hours after I left Shea's place. I looked at the caller ID. It was Shea. I ignored it. It rang again. I ignored it again. She kept calling and I never answered, not through the trip and not after I arrived home in California. I had nothing else to say to her. She'd made it clear that we were done, and I couldn't let myself get sucked back into the on-again, off-again game we'd played for the past year.

Shea

The moment Syd walked out the door I knew I'd made the biggest mistake of my life. Immediately I called the guy I had been dating and broke it off. Then I called Syd, but he wouldn't answer. I called again. He still didn't answer. I kept calling and calling and calling.

At one point I called my mom and told her what had happened. My mom loved Syd. He'd won her over on the first day we met when he'd asked for my number in front of her. She loved that he'd always cared for me so well and never was afraid to show it. She told me that all I could do was keep trying, so that's what I did. Austin still kept in touch with Syd, and although he never said anything, I knew he was rooting for us.

Finally, after two days and at least a hundred phone calls, Syd answered. He sounded cold when he said hello, but I didn't let that stop me. I told him I loved him and I apologized for taking him on this roller-coaster ride of emotions. I told him I wanted to be with him forever. I told him that he was my opposite and that was the reason I loved him so much. I had spent so many months analyzing why we weren't a good fit that I'd missed how our counterbalance made us a pair. "We make the best team," I said. It may take me a while to wrap my head around an idea, but once I do, I'm all in. Thankfully he came around. "You know I've always loved you. Please don't break my heart again," he told me.

My birthday was coming up, so I told him I wanted to fly down and spend that day with him. Since my birthday is July 5, that gave us the entire Fourth of July weekend together. I couldn't wait to see him.

I flew to Los Angeles on July 3. Syd had the entire weekend planned out for us. On the day I arrived, we went to the Santa Monica Pier. Something felt different that day. We'd always enjoyed being together, but knowing we were both in this for the long haul, wherever it took us, made me feel even more relaxed with Syd. At the end of the day, we rode the Ferris wheel on the pier so we could watch the sun melt into the ocean. We took pictures; we laughed; we were us.

"Close your eyes," Syd said. I had no idea what he had in mind, but I did what he asked. I heard him reaching into the camera bag and then he said, "Now open them." I opened my eyes, and he was down on one knee in the Ferris wheel car. "Will you marry me?" he asked, holding out a ring.

I did not hesitate for even a second. I loved Syd with my whole heart and never wanted to do anything without him by my side again. He was my best friend, my balance, and my confidant. Our juxtaposition of styles opened our eyes to new perspectives and added dimension to our lives. Neither of us had any idea what we were about to get ourselves into, but we were ready.

three

LIVE WITH WHAT YOU LOVE

| *Discover what truly inspires you.* |

Shea

It wasn't long after I had a ring on my finger that I shifted gears into wedding-planning mode. We had been living in different states for over a year now and both wanted a short engagement. I didn't want to get married in the winter or wait until the following summer, so we landed on a fall wedding.

I may not have been a designer at the time, but I knew from my extensive internet research that the first step to planning a wedding was putting together a mood board. I created a collage of images that spoke to me and carried them around in a plastic three-ring binder. This was my first attempt at nailing down my personal style and creating a feeling through design. I enlisted my mom's help, made lengthy checklists, exercised decisiveness, and planned everything fast—a skill set that would serve me well in the years to come. At twenty-three, I was swayed by too many trends, but I also learned that mixing old and new was (and still is) my jam.

We had a small wedding ceremony followed by a reception in a red barn with two hundred friends and family. Guests were greeted by two large willow wreaths hung on the outside of the sliding barn doors, with ochre-yellow silk ribbons trailing from each. As the night grew dark, you could see the café lights glowing in the rafters. The entry table was filled with a collection of vintage picture frames with old family wedding photos from our ancestors. My mom and I placed round tables throughout with natural linens and bicycle baskets filled with loosely arranged flowers as the centerpieces. The menu was less about presentation and more about comfort. The caterers passed prosciutto-wrapped asparagus, pesto paninis, and Syd's favorite, pecan pie squares. The DJ played from the hay loft, and Syd and I danced to Cat Power's "Sea of Love."

We rode away from our reception under a sea of fall leaves on a bicycle built for two. The leaves were changing, the air was crisp, and our cheeks hurt from smiling. Riding that vintage cobalt blue Schwinn Twinn together was the first of our many tests in teamwork.

Syd

Once I had successfully pulled off the engagement, I figured my job was to find a new suit and show up on time. Shea would take care of the rest. We may not have said our vows yet, but I knew her well enough to know that the girl knew what she wanted when she saw it. When she got a design vision in her head, it was best if I stayed away from color schemes and floral varieties (a lesson that has served me well to this day).

Our families made the journey to Utah from all over the country to celebrate our wedding day. It was a day to remember, but as a dude, I was mostly looking forward to the honeymoon.

Shea

Since we couldn't afford to pay for a moving van, the day after we got married we loaded all of my stuff into Syd's parents' RV and they hauled it down to Orange County for us. Whatever didn't fit in the motorhome we crammed into my VW Jetta, and then we drove straight from Salt Lake to LAX, with the exception of getting pulled over in the middle of the desert for speeding. Upon arrival, we parked and locked the car filled with my possessions and hopped on a plane to Mexico. Our honeymoon was dreamy—the weather was perfect, and so was the all-you-can-eat chips and guac. We had our first squabble as a married couple when Syd criticized my kayaking stroke and then I made him do all the work to get us back to the shore. Thankfully, we recovered from the kayak incident pretty quickly, and after a week in paradise, we returned home to the apartment where we were going to start our life together.

Syd

I like to think that Shea had a blank canvas when she moved into my one-bedroom apartment after our honeymoon. It was five hundred square feet, with a sliding glass door that led to a small patio on the balcony, and you could see the living room, dining nook, kitchen, and bedroom from the front door. The walls were cream but had yellowed from the previous tenants' cigarette smoke. I had a coffee table fashioned as a makeshift media console to house my TV and Xbox, and a mattress on the floor. The bedroom was so small that a full-size bed filled the entire room. It was a good thing we were newlyweds because there was a lot of cuddling.

I had one package of frozen orange chicken from Trader Joe's in the freezer and a bottle of sriracha in the fridge. There was no seating or a dresser or even a dining table. Shea had been to the apartment a few times, so she knew what she was getting into and had mentioned that I should at least get a couch. My brother's business partner, my other boss, was giving a bunch of stuff away, and I snagged a hot-pink George Foreman grill and a used white—well, mostly white—IKEA couch right before she moved in. Life to this point was all about going to work, chatting with my babe, then gaming late into the night.

Our first day together in our new apartment was just like our first day in every new home thereafter. We unpacked and organized, and then Shea started waving her arms about, pointing at light fixtures that "needed" to come down and walls that "needed" paint. I mostly ignored her until she'd ask, "Hey, can you do me a favor real quick? I'd love some help moving the furniture so I can paint." I was new to the game at this point, so I said sure without hesitation. Over a decade later, I know to ask what the favor is before agreeing to it. Paint is Shea's gateway to a slippery slope of home-improvement projects.

"It's the least expensive way to transform your home," she'd say.

"Now that we've done the walls, the cabinets look pretty blah, don't you think?"

"I can see what the space needs now—a big gallery wall."

"I found this dresser for a steal! It just needs to be refinished and it will be perfect. I've already ordered new hardware."

Shea has always had great vision, but she can't refinish a dresser to save her life. Through trial and error, we've learned that Shea's got ideas and I've got the patience to execute them.

Shea

Oh, I had ideas. The thing about our old apartment was that I never viewed it for what it was but what it could be. Seeing the potential that others could not yet see lit a fire within me. During that time I transitioned from reading wedding blogs to design blogs in my spare time. I would jump from one to the next, reading about pops of color and velvet upholstery and taking quizzes about discovering your personal style. I didn't know it yet, but this was my design school, and our apartment was my first project.

The owner gave us permission to do what we wanted *within reason*. I decided to start with paint because it seemed to be the project with the most bang for our buck. I had never chosen a paint color before, and doing something so "grown-up" excited me. At the time, gray walls were all the rage, and we put about six samples of paint on the wall. I could see that some pulled too purple or blue, and I settled on a dolphin-hued gray that felt just right. We painted all five hundred square feet, and the end result felt like magic. I was instantly hooked on the power of paint.

All my life I'd watched my mom make our home look great on a small budget, so I had some ideas about what to do. She repainted every square inch of my childhood home multiple times, scraped wallpaper until her fingers were raw, and helped me decorate my dorm space to make it the cutest on campus. If we could make a cinder block wall look good, I knew I could tackle this apartment.

This realization led to a change of heart about the hand-me-down white sectional. It just needed a little love. I filled it with pillows that I begged Syd to make for me. I have his mom to thank for his sewing lessons! I would find designer fabric remnants online and could only afford the front side of the pillow, so we kept an inexpensive roll of linen in our closet for the backs of the pillows.

Pretty soon we graduated from painting walls to spraying cabinetry and from plugging in lamps to rewiring chandeliers. Through this process we learned how to tackle home projects together, but it was about more than tools and painters' tape. We were learning how to work together and communicate, discovering our style as a couple.

Syd

We had a galley kitchen that was about seven feet long, with yellowing laminate cabinetry. Before we painted the walls, nothing stood out as bad because it was all bad. The minute the new light-gray paint had dried, I tried to pretend the kitchen cabinets looked good as they were, in the hopes that Shea wouldn't notice. But she always notices.

The next weekend I found myself out in the garage, painting the kitchen cabinets. Thankfully there were only six doors and three drawers in the entire kitchen, because after I had removed each cabinet front, taped everything off, and primed and painted them, they began to peel. Apparently, you need a special product to adhere to laminate, and that's not what I had used. On top of it all, Shea hated the color. "Too stark," she said. "I'm looking for a soft white." I was too mad to respond, but I knew she was right, which made me madder.

Shea has been convincing me to make sweat investments into our homes since the day we got married, and they always pay off. She transitioned our apartment from a mattress on the floor into a place that felt like home. Shea's designs overhauled the aesthetics, but also the mood when you were there. She showed me that rugs on the floor and art on the walls could be more than just stuff. It spoke to our interests, our personalities, and the way we lived. These changes inspired us to enjoy our time at home instead of avoiding it.

Shea

Something within my soul compels me to make my surroundings feel beautiful. From the cinder blocks in my dorm room to our first apartment, my eyes cannot rest until I've created an environment that feels calming. By the time I finished designing our apartment, it was completely transformed. The front door opened directly into the living room, and I created a faux entryway with hooks and artwork I framed myself. The dining room was now anchored by a classic white drum shade from Overstock.com, a round table I found on Craigslist, and upholstered linen chairs from the scratch-and-dent section of Pier 1 Imports. I elevated the IKEA couch with an eclectic combination of pillows and a large-scale gallery wall that spanned as high as our fourteen-foot vaulted ceiling. Syd's Xbox was now neatly hidden within a proper media console, and I had covered the stained carpet with a natural jute rug. I replaced all of the vertical blinds with panels and hardware I picked up at Target. Our bedroom still didn't have room for nightstands, but I saved for six months to purchase a simple square headboard and Schumacher pillows (well, only the front side). We managed to squeeze a dresser in the room, and it was so tight that you could sit at the foot of our bed and open it. I placed a round mirror above the dresser to make the space feel larger and used vintage treasures I'd found while thrifting to add the finishing touches to the space.

While redecorating our home, I was working for a marketing firm in Orange County. But I needed another creative outlet, so I started making headbands. Yes, headbands. It was in the handmade heyday, when there was a huge resurgence of crafting and Etsy reigned supreme. My mom and I opened an online shop called Old Soul, New Heart, and I used my PR skills to pitch our pieces to blogs. We set up a makeshift backdrop to photograph the products in our garage. Syd supported my new venture by taking pictures of me modeling the accessories, wearing a fancy top and PJ bottoms below the camera's line of sight.

My degree in PR came in handy, and we were featured on the *Today Show* and in a slew of national bridal magazines. I don't think we ever considered what to do if the press worked. The attention was exciting, but we were grossly underprepared and only knew how to put our heads down and work late into the night to make headbands, photograph them, and pack and ship orders. My mom was still in Texas, so we divided the styles between us and fulfilled the orders from both locations. She made more of the pieces so I could do the marketing and photography. We made everything ourselves and had no experience in scaling or sourcing, or in business in general. The grind of making each piece by hand and constantly putting money back into the business completely sucked the fun out of what was originally intended to be a creative outlet. The shop was only open for a little over a year, but it taught me a couple of valuable lessons: (1) telling a story and spreading the word through organic marketing works, and (2) cultivating the ability to scale and to outsource the manufacturing to capable hands was the way to do business.

I still cringe a little every time I wear a headband.

Syd

We didn't eat dinner on our table anymore because there were ribbons, sequins, and feathers everywhere. Shea worked tirelessly for months to make and fulfill orders for her new business, but it wasn't her calling in life. She didn't light up when we talked about it, and it was draining her creative energy rather than sparking it. She seemed discontent with both her day job and her side hustle but wasn't interested in my advice: "Why don't you design for people?"

"What people?" she'd say. "Why would anyone in their right mind pay me to design their home? I didn't go to design school, and my portfolio consists of a one-bedroom apartment filled with bargain-bin finds and hand-me-down furniture."

"Well, why don't you go to school?"

Her answer was always the same: "I can't draw."

Shea

It was the same excuse I told myself when I avoided taking a design class in college. I was terrified to try and perhaps discover I was terrible at the thing I wanted so desperately to be good at. I was afraid of failure, but also of success. I learned the hard way that burnout is real, and if we don't give ourselves the tools to progress, we end up treading water. With success came new challenges, and I didn't feel qualified to overcome them.

The glossy pages of my torn magazines were filled with natural light and fresh flowers and were styled to perfection, but what was happening behind the scenes? Was I chasing a dream that wasn't as dreamy as it sounded? What if my skills as a marketer outweighed my design capabilities and I didn't have the skills to back up what I was promoting? What if I was able to attract clients only to disappoint them with the end result?

I had already shuttered the doors of one business and couldn't bear the thought of doing it again. If I was going to change careers and subsequently my entire trajectory in life, I needed to be certain this was the right path for me. I did not want to continue taking a trial-and-error approach to discovering my calling in life. I wanted to leap out of bed every morning ready to pursue my passion. This was not a decision to take lightly, so I decided to take it one step at a time.

I received an advertisement in the mail one day for a community college close to us, and it clicked that this was the way to get my feet wet. Tuition was cheap, and there was little risk of embarrassment. I could take a few classes at my own pace and see where it led me.

Syd

I never saw anyone enjoy doing something like Shea enjoyed decorating our first apartment. Eventually we moved into a bigger apartment and she overhauled that interior too. When her friends called her for advice, she lit up. I could tell she longed to do more than make our apartments a decent place to live. She didn't talk about design like it was something she wanted to do on the side. This was her passion. It was clear to me that she'd quit her job in a second to design full-time.

I kept telling Shea, "What do you have to lose?" If she enrolled in design classes and sucked, so what? But I knew she wouldn't suck. I could see her natural talent. I knew what she was capable of. As for not being able to draw, I told her, "Big deal—just do it." We didn't have kids yet, and my job was going well. The timing felt right for her to explore making a change.

Shea

In my mind, a huge barrier stood between me and the world of design. I held on to insecurities about my lack of drawing skills and schooling and felt as if I'd be wasting my bachelor's degree if I tried something new. Having transformed a nearly empty, one-bedroom apartment into a livable space hardly qualified me to make the jump. Just thinking about calling myself an interior designer made me feel like an impostor. From PR to marketing to headbands, I fumbled to find a subject matter that inspired me. I wasn't confident that being passionate about style was enough to make a career change, but with Syd's encouragement, I finally went online and signed up for two classes: space planning and introduction to interior design. To allow more flexibility with my schedule, I took a new job as a part-time copywriter for a local marketing agency. My obsession with creating beautiful moments consumed me, and I wanted to live what I loved. I didn't know the rules or lingo—I just knew I loved design and wanted to spend my days creating environments that evoked a feeling.

four

EMBRACE THE PROCESS

*Confidence in your craft is built by
learning from one experience at a time.*

Shea

In design school, we sat at drafting tables with a large roll of
tracing paper where we would plot kitchen layouts and try to
remember how many feet were required between the refrigerator
and countertops. My drawings were one-dimensional and made
in black and white. I was learning the foundational elements of
creating spaces that met code requirements, but community college did not offer a course in developing personal style. I needed
an opportunity to create and discover my own style and couldn't
wait to have a home of our own to experiment on.

With each home project, I earned a design badge of sorts,
through making mistakes, discovering new resources, and solving problems. I would file away each experience, both good and
bad, so I could recall the information when tackling the next
design challenge. Layer upon layer I was building confidence as

a designer. At this point in my journey, I felt sure of my ability to make cosmetic decisions about things like colors and furniture.

After spending our first three years of marriage renting apartments, I wanted to paint a wall without having to ask for permission, and I was ready to smell some construction dust. I wasn't just looking for a place to live—I was looking for a project, a place where I could put my knowledge to the test and try out my talents and turn them into bona fide skills on my own dime before I began working with clients. I was in my second year of design school and motivated to execute ideas on more than tracing paper. I convinced Syd that all I needed was one good project to give me the runway I needed to launch my design business.

It was 2011, and the real estate market in Orange County had taken a huge hit. The only houses in our price range were short sales and foreclosures, which meant the prices were good but the competition was fierce. As soon as a house went on the market, an investor would swoop in with an all-cash offer. After a while Syd and I became disheartened. We thought we'd never find anything, and then, early one morning I came across a house. I called our real estate agent, who took us over to see it right away. The moment we drove up I knew this home was the one.

It was a two-story, beige stucco tract house with a tile roof and a rickety Juliet balcony (you know, one of those fake balconies you can only put flowers on) overlooking a faded garage door. It looked like every other home in the neighborhood, but the location was what spoke to me. The house was situated at the back of a cul-de-sac against a grassy hill, and I could see the fence line enclosing what appeared to be a rather large yard, which was unusual for the area. We followed our agent under an overgrown tree humming with bees and through a heavy wood gate. When we entered the home we were greeted by a partially eaten bagel on the table and four other couples already scoping out the property.

The price was within our budget, and even though its faux Tuscan style was out-of-date, the counters were sticky, and the previous owners had let the house fall into disrepair before it was foreclosed on, the property had potential. I'd been dreaming about the opportunity to fix up something, and that made this house—our house—the perfect place for me to turn the ideas keeping me up at night into reality. I could do it, and I was ready to prove myself.

Syd and I told the agent we'd take it before we even saw the second floor. By some small miracle, our offer was accepted, and after thirty days of holding our breath through escrow, the home was ours.

Syd

We closed on the house on December 23 and moved in the next day. We spent the entire day unpacking, cleaning, and arranging what little furniture we owned. When we finished, the two of us fell back on the sofa, exhausted. That's when we realized what day it was: December 24, Christmas Eve. Shea looked at me and said, "We need a tree!" I assumed all the tree lots were closed, but Shea said we had to try. I grabbed my coat and ran out the door.

By the time I left our house, it was already after six thirty in the evening, but I drove to the closest Christmas tree lot and hoped they'd still be open. I glanced at my watch, and it was about five minutes before seven. I yelled at the workers to wait as they were closing the gates. "I just need one. Just give me whatever!" And that's what they gave me—whatever. But I didn't care because I was in a hurry to get home and they were in a hurry for me to leave. I paid for my tree, threw it in the back of my pickup, and drove home. I hauled the tree into the house, and the first thing Shea asked was, "Did you get a stand?"

Oh crap. A stand. I hadn't even thought about that. The tree did have a couple of pieces of wood nailed to the bottom, which had helped it sort of stand up in the lot, so I stood the tree in the corner. It started leaning and was about to fall over when I shoved it and propped it against the wall. We didn't have any lights or ornaments to decorate with, but the Christmas tree was beautiful to us because it was our first one in our new home.

In true Shea fashion, about a week later she dove headfirst into the home renovation. And she wasn't talking a few cans of paint. Shea wanted to redo the kitchen. She told me that remodeling the home would be a "good investment" in the start of her design business and convinced me to remodel in stages, one room at a time. I was okay with working in phases and had already learned in our few short years of marriage that (1) there is no stopping Shea when she gets an idea in her head, and (2) there is no stopping Shea when she gets an idea in her head. Experience also had taught me that the upgrades would inevitably cost more than she estimated but the end result would be worth it.

Shea

In the four weeks leading to the closing on our home, I planned our new kitchen during packing breaks. After we moved in, we quickly settled (we didn't have much to unpack), and a few days later I brought in a crew for a quote to demo the kitchen. It was a U-shape layout with an island in the middle and a window above the sink, overlooking the backyard. The open-concept kitchen, dining room, and living room were in a row at the back of the house, with French doors behind our round kitchen table.

When we'd walked through the home the first time, I'd thought the open floor plan was perfect for a young family—no walls had to be knocked down or appliances moved. On the other hand, the finishes desperately needed updating. The kitchen floor had peach porcelain tiles, and I wanted to replace them with stained hardwood floors. When the first estimate for the demo came in at $500, Syd decided to do it himself. My long history of failed do-it-yourself (DIY) projects told me this was a terrible idea, but Syd tends to think he can do anything.

Syd

If I'm going to spend $500, I'm going to spend it on a new surfboard—not ripping out tile. I've always considered myself pretty handy. One project at a time I was stepping up my DIY game and feeling more confident for the next. I did these DIY projects not only for Shea but for her dad as well. He has this way of getting me to do stuff. As Shea mentioned earlier, he's a former FBI agent and SWAT team member. We've developed a close relationship over the years, and I'm quick to say yes to him. He grew up on a farm in North Carolina and has this deceptively calm demeanor and sweet Southern drawl. But I'm sure at any moment he could break my neck if he wanted to. He'll ask me to give him a hand, and by give him a hand, he means do it for him. I don't mind. I love to help.

In the short time Shea and I had been married, I'd amassed a collection of tools and completed my share of DIY projects. So when Shea mentioned the tile, I didn't think it would be a big deal. I mean, you throw around a sledgehammer and take out the trash, right?

Before I started tearing out tile I watched a how-to video on YouTube, then headed down to Home Depot to buy some tools. I discovered a handheld jackhammer that you could rent and was told that it was made for such a job. *Perfect. This is going to take an hour max, and then I'll go surf*, I thought. *Give me the right tool and I can do anything.* When I returned to the house I fired up the jackhammer and went to town on the tile. Dust and bits of tile flew everywhere. Even though I wore safety glasses, debris attacked my eyes. My entire body shook with the hammer until I could barely hang on to it.

After what seemed like forever (in reality probably twenty-five minutes), I stopped hammering. I'd removed part of one tile. One. Freaking. Tile.

Suddenly I was okay with spending $500 to have the tile removed. I played it cool with Shea and told her I didn't want to spend my weekend removing the tile and thought it would be a more efficient use of my time to focus on my real job at my brother's affiliate marketing company.

I don't think I was fooling her, but she was kind enough to pretend I was.

Shea

Even before Syd's battle with the kitchen tile, I felt certain the remodel couldn't be DIY. At the time, DIY was popular on home-improvement shows and design blogs, but the results always fell short of the look I wanted. Doing things ourselves like hanging lights and redoing cabinets in our small apartments made sense. But not in our forever home. I wanted this house to look and feel elevated, like the spaces I studied in design magazines. But my design taste has always outweighed my bank account, and I needed to find a way to make my budget stretch.

Though I thought Syd was covering up his failed tile removal attempt, he really was working so many hours that taking time off to remodel our entire home wasn't an option. We believed this was the home where we'd raise our future children, and there was no way I was going to convince Syd to remodel again anytime soon, so we needed to get it right the first time.

I had no prior kitchen remodeling experience, which was exactly what made me want to try. I believed it was a rite of passage into the design world. Our kitchen was the perfect place to try out my ideas without getting in over my head. The home was in good condition, but the builder-grade finishes were dated. I couldn't completely rip out everything and start over without having the kitchen eat up my entire budget for the house, but I also wanted something more custom to truly make my mark.

The cabinets were painted brown and topped with speckled granite, common in tract homes. There was a one-foot gap between the top of the upper cabinetry and the ceiling, where the previous owners left behind dust and baskets of trailing fake ivy. To save money, I'd reface the cabinets with white paint and add Shaker-style doors and new trim. Although I was working with much of the existing cabinetry, I needed to choose a few places to incorporate custom details that moved the kitchen away from its cookie-cutter roots.

I planned to incorporate an inexpensive, glossy white subway tile and take it a step beyond the typical backsplash. Instead of spending money to add a second row of cabinetry to bridge the gap to the ceiling, my vision was to extend the tile all the way to the ceiling around the room, to help distract from the short cabinets. I would swap the fan above the stove for a custom vent hood and replace the lone cabinet next to my new farmhouse sink with open shelves.

I ordered the hardware, a mix of polished nickel cup pulls and knobs, weeks before we had a cabinetmaker. The slightest details, like deciding between 1-inch and 1.25-inch knobs, exhilarated me.

The kitchen had a few existing can lights but lacked the "wow factor" that fixtures have on a space. Instead of installing the typical two pendants above our island, I wanted to take a risk and hang one oversized arch-top lantern.

I had my heart set on a classic white kitchen with Carrara marble countertops. Although a white kitchen may seem like an obvious choice now, back then it was a fresh look in a sea of Tuscan. Marble counters were a key element of the design; however, in my research I learned that marble was porous and harder to keep clean. But that did not deter me. When Syd questioned my choice of marble because it isn't as durable as other materials, I told him the ancient Greeks and Italians had been using marble for centuries. "If they can use it in Europe for hundreds and hundreds of years, then it's good enough for us," I said. That settled it, at least with Syd.

I envisioned how I wanted the kitchen to look and feel, but we couldn't execute this project on our own. That meant only one thing: I had to find a contractor. I started googling cabinet people in Orange County, but everyone I called wanted to build my cabinets from scratch. No one wanted to reface my existing cabinetry. A job that small didn't pay enough to make it worth their while. Discouraged, I started asking around to see if anyone had a reference for a carpenter who did quality yet affordable work. In Orange County, that was a hard combination to find.

Syd

My thrifty parents had just the guy for us. "You need to call John. He's done work for us for years," they said. "He's really handy and can do about anything." If my parents used him, he had to be doing work for a reasonable price.

They gave me his number, even though they weren't sure if he was still around. I called and he didn't answer, but his voice mail recording said, "This is John. Have a happy day!" This was the first clue that John wasn't a typical construction guy. In fact, there was nothing typical about him at all. He was more of a nomad carpenter who lived out of his station wagon. He worked for the bigger contractors we couldn't afford, but on the side he also did lots of small jobs like ours. When he returned my call he said he loved my parents and that, sure, he'd do whatever we needed.

The next Saturday morning at seven, he pulled up to our house, kicking up a cloud of sawdust and then opening his trunk. Through our upstairs window I could see a ladder strapped to the roof of his car and scrap pieces of millwork, tools, and a table saw in the back. He was wearing a white undershirt and carried a trucker mug of what I later learned was Mountain Dew.

I ran downstairs to let him in and he immediately started

chatting. Clearly the Mountain Dew was already working. "How's your mom? How's your dad? Nice house. Does your brother still live around the corner? I did a nine-inch crown for them a few years ago." John liked to talk, and I soon found that just saying hello usually reminded him of a story, and that story would turn into an hour-long conversation.

But when he shifted gears to work, he rarely took long breaks and was quick. He was resourceful as well, often looking out for cost-saving opportunities even more than we were. John became our liaison into the world of construction and didn't take advantage of us, even though we were easy targets. He was patient with us as we asked questions every step of the way and was such a pleasant guy that we almost didn't mind that he always made us late for everything. He also ended every conversation with, "Have a happy day!"

The first meeting at our home he asked us to walk him through our plans. Shea outlined her vision for the kitchen, and I stayed around to talk cost. He asked about things like molding profiles and dimensions of the open shelves. Evidently there was a discrepancy between our designs on paper and how contractors would interpret them. We didn't have answers for many of his questions, but he presented our options and helped nail down the details needed to bring Shea's designs to life.

Because it was our own home, there was no pressure or embarrassment that we were grossly underprepared for the meeting. I could see Shea taking mental notes of every nuance she had missed so she wouldn't overlook those specifications in the future. Without having the experience to discover our lack of experience, we never would have had the opportunity for growth.

Shea

When we first met with John, I told him I wanted to start with the cabinets. "No, you don't want to do that," he said. When I asked why, he explained that we needed to start with the floors, then move to the cabinets. "If you do the cabinets first, the flooring guys will damage them during installation." While he redid the cabinets, he said I needed to select my countertops and order them so they'd be available for installation at the right time. Since I'd never remodeled a kitchen before, I listened. John had a lot of experience and knew what he was doing. He helped me understand how to organize a remodel. He also pointed me to places where I could source materials and connected me with other subcontractors who took smaller jobs like ours in their spare time.

John also taught me to stand up for myself as a designer. When I shared my plans for the kitchen, he questioned my choices. "Are you sure you want to remove that cabinet? You're not going to be able to store anything with those open shelves."

"I know, but I want the display, and my dishes are pretty enough to set out," I pushed back.

Then he questioned my choice of Carrara marble for the countertops. "Why are you doing marble? You know it stains and scratches. What about quartz? Quartz is great."

"I know, but I want marble because I want marble," I said.

"But why?"

Then the tile guys came in and did the same thing: "You sure you want your backsplash in a brick pattern? People don't usually bring the tile to the ceiling. Don't you want to do a herringbone pattern?"

"No. I want a brick lay."

"You sure about that?"

At first all of the questions took me aback. I began to doubt myself. But spending more time thinking through my choices reinforced my reasons for wanting them. The more pushback I received from different contractors who came to work on our house, the more confident I became. I learned to consider the why behind decisions and to delve deeper than the superficial reason "because it looks good."

This process prepared me for client projects and taught me how to give my rationale behind certain selections. With each decision and explanation, I grew into my own as a designer, learning to trust my instincts but also to listen when I had an opportunity to learn.

John was the perfect guy to teach me these lessons. He challenged my choices but was still respectful, and ultimately he helped me bring to life dozens of design projects in my first year of business.

Syd

During the first part of the home remodel, we spent months washing dishes in the bathroom sink and eating pizza and Chinese takeout. All of the bedrooms were upstairs, so Shea and I sealed off the stairs with plastic and only went downstairs if we needed to leave the house. This kitchen remodel didn't come with a big reveal like you see on television. Instead, it was more of a slow reveal. The floors came first, and they looked great, but then the painters covered them up while the crew finished the cabinets and countertops. Then came the cabinet reveal, which looked awesome. Shea posted photos on Instagram throughout the process, which would eventually lead to her landing her first paid design job with the bookshelves.

I have never pretended to be a design expert, but what stood out the most to me was how beautiful she made the space while maintaining a feeling of comfort and livability. I wanted to be in the kitchen. It felt like home. It didn't feel like I was going to break something, although Shea did freak out a little if I left something, like a cut lemon, on the marble countertop. I imagined us spending many years eating around the island and watching our kids play in the backyard through the window above the kitchen sink.

This kitchen was the beginning of our journey together managing projects as a team. Shea conceptualized the design, and I facilitated the process behind the scenes.

As soon as the kitchen was done, she jumped into the living room. None of this was work to her; she lit up as she moved from one room to the other. I would watch her sit in empty rooms and stare at them, mentally assembling the pieces of her design puzzle. I had no doubt not only that she could do this for a living but that she'd kill it when she did.

Shea

Redoing our house wasn't just about creating a place for us to live and start a family. It was my portfolio, my way of launching my design career. In my PR work I enjoyed developing creative strategies but struggled to promote products I didn't feel passionate about. Now it was time to promote my work and my passion.

Initially I posted progress photos of our remodel on my

personal Instagram account in between photos of our trips to the beach. I posted pictures of my shoes on our new hardwood floors and swatches on our walls, and I soon noticed that home progress posts received significantly more engagement from friends than any of my other photos. After a few posts documenting our home remodel, I was hired to style the built-ins that started everything.

The day I styled the built-ins, I hopped off the ladder to step back and admire my work, then set up my SLR (single-lens reflex) camera and snapped a few pictures. I hadn't used that camera since my mom and I owned our hair accessory business, and I had only taken a one-day photography course to learn how to use the manual camera settings. I didn't have a tripod, so I held my breath and set a slow exposure to capture the natural light.

I am by no means a professional photographer, but I have picked up a few basic principles from analyzing interior photos over the years: Leave the lights off and let the sunshine illuminate the room. Pay attention to horizon lines to avoid the real estate bubble effect. Real estate photos use wide lenses to make rooms appear larger, but the result is impersonal and less engaging than a closer vignette. And stay away from filters and instead capture the true colors of a space.

My marketing experience taught me that photos have the ability to shape our emotions. With the right eye, a stack of plates and a bowl of fruit can be transformed into something spectacular. After shooting my clients' built-ins, I went home, sat cross-legged on our bed, and uploaded the photos to my laptop. I brightened the light, cropped out the printer in the photo, and added a hint of contrast. I was so excited I posted them to my personal Instagram the same evening, with the message, "Sneak peek of one of my client projects!"

A positive response to one photo was all I needed to gather the courage to launch my business. Instagram profiles were free, and setting up a separate account for Shea McGee Design seemed like a natural way to share my capabilities with potential clients, beyond my friend network. At the time only a handful of designers were using Instagram as a marketing tool, so I mostly sought out home decor brands and fashion bloggers for inspiration.

Syd

Within the first few weeks, Shea saw her following increase by the hundreds and even thousands. No leaders or models existed to pattern after in the interior design world, so Shea and I examined other industries to study how they were growing. We observed one consistent theme: consistency. Committing to making at least one post a day over the course of months and years was how you built a following, so Shea committed herself to posting once a day, even if she didn't have new projects to share.

We brainstormed ways to creatively stretch content across multiple posts. What could have been one post about a living room turned into ten: Shea's hands placing fabric on a design board, progress shot, shopping for flowers, sneak peek, before/after, half room, coffee table vignette, full-room view from different angles.

I listened to entrepreneur podcasts regularly in an effort to help Shea, but also because I had secretly begun to think about striking out on my own as well.

Shea

A couple of weeks after posting the built-ins and launching my design account on Instagram, the text messages began rolling in. "I hear you're designing now. I need some help!" With a few semesters of design school, experience with our own home, and one client project under my belt, I was ready to call myself a designer. The confidence to pursue my passion didn't come overnight or with a certificate on my wall. It was built by having the courage to study, make mistakes, and channel experiences into personal growth.

five

GROUND YOUR SPACE

*Use foundational pieces with scale and
weight to create an inspired room.*

Syd

Shea and I always dreamed of having kids, but we agreed that we wanted a few years of just the two of us first. We married young and wanted to establish our careers, become more financially stable, and have the freedom to do what we wanted when we wanted before a couple of little hooligans took it all away. The boxes were now checked, and we both felt it was the right time to start our family.

We were in the middle of remodeling our home, and Shea already had designated an upstairs bedroom, the one closest to the master suite, as the future nursery. I was still running operations for my brother's company, and Shea was still working part-time for a marketing agency, attending design school, and starting to build a clientele for her interior design business.

For a year we got our hopes up every month, only to see a

negative sign on the pregnancy test. Eventually I stopped asking for updates, knowing Shea would tell me when she had good news to share.

On the Fourth of July weekend, the same weekend we got engaged four years prior, I left the office early to meet with Shea and ride our beach cruisers from San Clemente to Dana Point. A two-lane bike path connects the towns, so you can watch both fireworks shows as they shoot them off a pier and into the ocean. It was late, but the sky sparkled.

Shea casually leaned over to me and said, "Guess what?"

"What?"

"I'm pregnant!"

I pulled over and stopped my bike. "Are you kidding me?" Her huge smile told me she wasn't joking. We hugged and cried joyous tears because we were in this together, and the wait had made the destination even sweeter. While pedaling home, I let go of the handlebars, looked to the sky, and stretched my arms out wide. I thought of all the adventures I'd share with my new little buddy. We'd surf, skate, and build forts in our new backyard.

Shea

I don't like secrets, and I especially don't like to keep secrets from Syd. We have an honest—almost too honest—dynamic in our relationship that keeps us connected. He tells me when he doesn't like my haircut, and I tell him when his ideas are too crazy. He has always been my best friend and partner. And best friends share in the good and the bad.

The five-hour wait between seeing a positive test in our

bathroom to sharing the results with Syd felt like an eternity. When I leaned over on my cruiser to tell Syd the news, I couldn't keep a straight face. It was really happening! We were going to be parents, and I knew Syd would be the best dad.

Syd slides down every banister he sees, jumps off rocks, and eats ice cream for breakfast when he feels like it. Because he was the youngest of six kids, I had seen him in his Uncle Syd role with at least a dozen nieces and nephews, and they adored him. I knew our baby would feel the same.

Within a few weeks of finding out I was pregnant, the morning sickness kicked in (all day, every day), and something had to give. I prioritized what I felt most passionate about: my design business. I didn't even tell my professors; I just never again showed up in class.

I put in my two-weeks' notice and wrapped up my last few projects with the ad agency and focused all the attention I could muster on getting through the first trimester and building my portfolio. The flexibility to design from my sofa while wearing sweatpants and posting to Instagram was exactly what I needed during this time.

As the nausea lifted, my energy bounced back, and I was dedicated to laying the foundation for my business. There was a steep learning curve to the operational components behind the scenes; purchase orders, billing, contracts, and invoicing consumed most of my days. I was elated when I finally had time to create for clients. I've always been most creative in the evenings, so I'd focus on the administrative tasks during the day and brainstorm design and marketing ideas late into the night. The design portion of my evening involved compiling pillow combinations, drawing cabinetry, and curating design boards. Then I'd put on my marketing cap and edit photos, post design tips on my blog to gain credibility, and comment on other Instagram accounts so like-minded design enthusiasts could discover me.

Syd and I were both hunkered down and focused on building businesses, but the difference was that for me, the work didn't feel like work.

Syd

I had a small desk next to our bed, and I spent more time there than I did sleeping. Before work, after work, and in the middle of the night, I was at that desk.

Most mornings I was there by five thirty or six to check on projects before I went to the office. I'd sit in traffic for an hour before arriving home to eat dinner with Shea and was back at the desk again until midnight, and once more at three in the morning to check on ad campaigns, before waking and following the same routine all over again. I had allowed work to become my life.

And it wasn't because the work was my passion. Becoming engrossed in a start-up doesn't happen because you consciously decide to let it overtake you. It happens because, like infants, start-ups are fragile and need constant nourishment. Every problem that arises has the potential to ruin the company, and I was determined to prove myself.

Although I never vocalized my true feelings, I had a chip on my shoulder about not finishing college and was driven to prove to the world, and to Shea, that I could succeed without a diploma on my wall. However, I wasn't surfing or riding my bike. I wasn't doing anything that invigorated me.

When I first took the job, I bought into the idea of building the company from the ground up and the "all hands on deck" mentality it took to make the business successful. I was motivated by being an underdog, rallying my teams to be scrappy and rise to the occasion.

My tenacity and resourcefulness paid off. In a few short years, we grew from one employee, me, to twenty-five employees. My brother, his business partner, and I started in a one-room office next door to a liquor store in a sketchy part of town. We left the mini blinds closed day and night so passersby wouldn't be tempted to steal our computer equipment. We'd gone from hoping we'd make a few bucks off of email campaigns to building proprietary technologies and a multimillion-dollar company in an office with valet parking and an ocean view. We'd partnered with an international agency, increased our global footprint, and exceeded our revenue goals.

But after spending years of rolling out of bed to sit at that desk during all hours of the night, I was burned out. With a baby on the way, I couldn't keep sacrificing my relationships for this job. Not only was working with family taking its toll, but Shea and I rarely saw each other. The company was growing and nobody wanted to take their foot off the accelerator, but I couldn't stop thinking about creating something of my own.

Shea

Before we even purchased our house, I spent a lot of time wandering around the Laguna Design Center, looking at wallpaper and textiles for inspiration. Then I discovered I could take home free wallpaper samples, and most days I came home with an armful. I'm sure the free swatches were intended for designers with long client rosters and fabric libraries, but I hoarded them like candy.

I used a few for school presentations and stored the rest in wire bins so I could practice pairing pattern and color combinations.

One day I was wandering up and down the aisles, looking at wallpaper, and I stopped in my tracks. The most beautiful pastel paper with hummingbirds was staring back at me.

I wanted to name my future daughter after the wren, a small bird that symbolizes joy in life, and here was this amazing wallpaper with hummingbirds. It felt serendipitous.

However, once we started designing the nursery, I couldn't stop there. Since one room flowed into another, how could I not do the rest of the upstairs as well? With Wren's due date approaching, we didn't have much time to finish. Our "remodel in stages" plan became "let's finish this as quickly as we can." The kitchen, family room, and dining room were done, so we dove into the upstairs bedrooms all at once. The work upstairs was minimal compared to the main floor, and we painted our master bedroom, the nursery, and the spare bedroom, which would be used as a shared office.

I sold Syd on the idea by telling him that if we did the entire upstairs, we could finally dispose of the rest of the brown shag carpeting that covered our house.

Syd

Oh man, I hated that carpet. It wasn't just hideous. The shag was so long that I'd walk down the hall barefoot, half asleep, and *bam!* I'd step on a Lego. And we didn't even have kids yet! The Legos were from the previous owner, or maybe the owner before that. Who knows how long those deadly plastic landmines had been buried down there? It didn't even matter how often you vacuumed.

And if you dropped any change on the carpet, forget it. It was gone forever. Everything disappeared once it hit that carpet.

We ripped out the carpet downstairs when we redid the living room and family room, but we couldn't afford to redo all the floors in the house yet, so we'd lived with it. When Shea said we could rip out the rest of the carpet if we redid the whole upstairs, I was like, "Let's get started today. Right now." I'd never been so happy to get rid of something.

The carpet did get one last shot of revenge, however. When we had the kitchen cabinets painted, the crew said they'd give us a deal if we hired them to paint all of the interior trim at the same time, including the upstairs.

Seven months later, when we ripped out the carpet, a stripe of the old paint ran along the bottom of all the baseboards. The height of the shag carpet had prevented them from painting the entire baseboard properly. That was the day we learned to tear out the carpet before painting the baseboards.

Since Shea was already stretching our budget, we couldn't afford to have the painters come back and fix the stripe, so we left it throughout the entire upstairs. It may be there to this day, for all we know. The spirit of the shag carpeting lives on in that unpainted stripe. At least the people who live there now don't have to worry about stepping on old Legos. Though they might be missing out on finding some loose change.

Shea

We replaced the carpet with a cream Berber carpet. I've always been a fan of carpet that acts as a backdrop for the furniture so the other finishes can shine. The carpet was in, the paint was dry, and the walls were a blank canvas.

When embarking on a new room design, I search until I find something that piques my interest and is strong enough visually to set the tone for the entire space. This foundational decision serves as a jumping-off point for every decision thereafter. Sometimes it's a rug, a pillow, or a piece of art. In this case it was the hummingbird wallpaper, which would be the central element in the space. Each choice would complement or tie into the inspiration.

The wallpaper was an iconic English paper, with a duck egg–blue background and painterly jewel-toned birds fluttering around blossoming branches. While the organic movement throughout the pattern was lovely, I didn't want the room to feel busy, so I hired our carpenter, John, to build wainscot halfway up the wall, and I painted it white to match the baseboards. The wallpaper was positioned above the wainscot, and I appreciated that the installer took great care to match all the seams.

I ordered a simple empire chandelier, with swooping strings of clear beads finished off with a matte gray metal tassel in the center. Syd installed the light fixture with one chain link, because the ceilings were only eight feet high. When he stood on the ladder to hold up the chandelier, we discovered there was only one inch remaining before breaking my seven-foot clearance rule. When you hang a light lower than seven feet, it's a visual distraction and also dangerous.

With the colorful birds on the walls, to achieve the calming atmosphere I envisioned I needed to keep the furnishings simple. I centered a white crib with mid-century-style legs between two windows on the back wall and placed a vintage gold leaf mirror above the crib. I made sure Syd used an anchor with a three-hundred-pound capacity to steady the ten-pound mirror.

I waited eight weeks for my glider to arrive, upholstered with a custom fabric that looked like linen but performed like steel. I angled it in the back corner next to the crib and placed a sea green garden stool next to it because I imagined myself spending a lot of time in that chair and I needed a place to rest a bottle or phone.

Even though the room already had wall-to-wall carpet, I wanted the nursery to feel extra plush and cozy, so I placed an oversized, white sheepskin rug in the middle of the room to ground the space and tie together the furniture on opposite sides of the room. A French gray dresser with dark ring pulls doubled as clothing storage and a changing table.

The finishing touch to the room was a forty-inch-square painting I commissioned of an abstract blush tutu. It tied in the hints of pink on the hummingbirds, and having taken dance lessons while growing up, I hoped to instill the same love in my daughter.

A few weeks before my due date, Syd finished assembling the crib. He also had to take the door off the frame to get the glider in the room.

Every vignette had been carefully crafted, and the nursery was very photogenic. I waited for a sunny day to open the shutters and take pictures for my portfolio and to share on social media. I posted the photos to Instagram, my blog, and Pinterest. Within a few days, I received an email from a decor blog with millions of readers, who asked me for an interview and for permission to share Wren's nursery tour.

The bookshelves had been a hit with friends, and our kitchen had attracted potential clients. But the nursery went viral. It was pinned, tagged, shared, and reposted thousands of times. The momentum was building, and my Instagram account was gaining major traction.

Syd

Shea would set milestones for her Instagram account. The first goal was to reach one thousand followers, and the next climb was to ten thousand. I told her that when she reached ten thousand followers, we'd celebrate with a staycation in Laguna Beach.

I was invested in the success of Shea's Instagram account. We'd spend hours discussing how to crack the code and analyzing what made certain strategies more successful than others. I'd listen to social media marketing podcasts and share what I learned, and she'd run with it. We were genuinely curious about what images and captions spoke to people and wanted to understand why. If a post bombed, we weren't discouraged—we just tried something new the next time. Did our followers engage more during certain times of the day? Did a spike in followers occur if we posted a picture of a full room versus a cropped vignette?

One day I snapped a picture of Shea laying out a gallery wall on our living room floor. She carefully arranged every framed piece, doing a test run of her vision before taking it to a client's house for installation. I took a photo of the entire room because she had overtaken it and that was the only way I could capture the whole scene, but the angle was actually quite artistic, and she decided to post it. We didn't anticipate the positive reaction it received, and after some trial and error we realized that wide photos incorporating design and featuring Shea perform better than tightly cropped photos of her without a home scene in the background.

An increase in followers, likes, and comments were measurable metrics with instant gratification. We were hooked on the feedback loop and better understanding both the platform and her audience. We were establishing the groundwork for what would eventually become the most valuable tool in our business.

Shea would check in and monitor her feed every hour or so. She was just shy of her goal of reaching ten thousand followers when she leaned over with both elbows on the kitchen island to squint at her iPhone screen. "So many questions about everything all the time!" she said, annoyed. "What paint color is that? Where is that chair from? How often do you water your fiddle-leaf fig tree?"

"Well, why don't you answer them?" I asked.

"Because real designers don't give away their secrets. None of the other designers I follow answer their followers' questions."

I suggested that perhaps she should be the designer to change that. I was following influencers in the workout industry who were sharing free workout tips, a strategy that led to huge growth to their businesses. I could see that providing value for free also reaped rewards in other ways. When professionals share their knowledge, they establish themselves as the expert and develop a closer connection with their audience. Shea hesitated but agreed to give it a shot.

Within a few weeks of responding and sharing, I could see her perspective on social media engagement had completely changed. "You were right—it's working!" she said. "The people aren't just numbers, and I'm connecting with them on a different level."

I then wrote in my journal: *Shea said I was right.*

Her growth trajectory continued upward, and she soon reached ten thousand followers. I booked a room in downtown Laguna Beach, and we spent an evening walking down Pacific

Coast Highway, past tchotchke shops with shells hanging in the windows, to a hidden alleyway that smelled of waffle cones. We sat on a stoop and talked under the crisscrossed lights while indulging in dulce de leche gelato from our favorite ice cream shop. I continued to be her sounding board as we entered new territory together.

Shea

I was thirty-nine weeks pregnant and still taking on design clients but planned to take a break from everything after the baby was born. I wanted to focus solely on figuring out how to be a mom. Eventually I'd start doing design work again, but I wanted to ease back into it.

My due date came and went. My feet were swollen, and I was miserable. Three days after my due date, I went for a walk on the San Clemente beach trail, hoping that might trigger labor. It did. As soon as my contractions started, Syd and I rushed to the hospital. They took me back and checked me out.

"It's going to be a while," they told me. "You might as well go home."

However, my gut told me something wasn't right. Call it mother's intuition, but I had this overwhelming sense that leaving the hospital would be a huge mistake.

"I'm not leaving," I said.

I was so adamant they finally agreed to do an ultrasound to make sure the baby was fine. They discovered that our baby girl was doing gymnastics (and she hasn't stopped since). But she was also breech and sunny-side up, making it impossible for me to dilate. All the while, my labor pains got stronger and stronger.

The staff had me walk the halls and do awkward stretches to coax our baby girl to flip, but nothing worked. As soon as I was ready to start pushing, I knew something was very wrong. Everyone started rushing around the room. The baby's heart rate suddenly dropped, and so did mine. Syd's face was somber as he leaned over the side of the hospital bed to kiss my forehead and squeeze my hand.

One of the nurses shoved some papers in front of me to sign. As soon as I did, they whisked me out of the birthing room and into the OR for an emergency C-section. My body was numbed, but my mind was alert to the panic in the room. I coped by focusing on Syd as the doctors and nurses shouted commands around us. He is always by my side when I need him most, encouraging me to press forward when I doubt my own strength.

The next thing I remember was hearing our baby girl cry and then seeing her tiny red head in a picture on Syd's phone. I was so happy to hear her squawking, yet sad that I couldn't immediately hold her.

Everything was a blur until the doctors brought her in, bundled like a little burrito, and I felt all six pounds, six ounces of her warm body against mine. I could feel her presence grounding me and pushing me to fulfill a new calling in life.

My first few weeks (okay, months) of motherhood felt like survival. I was completely overwhelmed and desperate to feel like myself again. I'd sit in Wren's nursery, rocking and nursing her, with tears streaming down my face. I remember thinking, *Is this my new normal?*

Thankfully, I realized soon enough that allowing myself the space to create made me fall in love with my role as a mother.

Within a few weeks, still hunched over as I recovered from

the C-section, I was carrying Wren in her car seat to jobsites as I wrapped up a couple of lingering projects.

Design is the outlet that gives me the frame of mind to be present for the most important people in my life. And soon it would bolster us during the most trying year of our marriage.

Syd

On our way home from the hospital after Wren was born, Shea rode in the back seat with our baby girl to make sure she stayed alive on our drive home. When we walked in, we were happy to be back in our own home after days of fluorescent hospital lights and the rhythmic beeping of monitors.

I was running a few hours late in sending out email campaigns, so I opened my laptop on the kitchen table and used my foot to rock Wren's car seat on the floor while Shea took a much-needed nap. The change of scenery felt nice, and it occurred to me that perhaps a change of scenery at work would do me some good as well.

I started to outline a plan for the transition from working for my brother to running my own affiliate marketing business. My demanding work schedule left little time for Shea and our new baby, so I saw entrepreneurship as an opportunity to be home more. My relationship with my brother became tense as my requests to take breaks on evenings and weekends were denied. The boundaries between work and family were blurred, and professional matters became personal. I could run a lean operation by doing most of the work myself, along with one partner, but I needed to buy servers. We had gone through most of our financial reserves finishing the home remodel, but that was fine, since we needed to finish it before the baby came. (Although I still think Shea may have hustled me with the whole "remodel in stages" idea.) I purchased about $20,000 in servers, depleting the rest of our savings, and put the rest on a credit card, to start laying the groundwork for my business.

About two months after Wren was born, I listened to the Killers on my way to work and sat at my desk, like I did every other day. Being there confirmed everything I already knew: I wanted to strike out on my own and didn't want to wait any longer. On the spot, I decided to talk to my brother. I stood up, pushed my chair back, and went to his office. When I walked in, I shut the door behind me and told him that it had been a good run, but I was ready to make the move to working for myself. Our Irish blood runs hot, and he wasn't interested in a transition plan. "Get out of my office and never come back," he said, but with a few more expletives. Time has mended our relationship, but that day was hell.

Clearing my desk and leaving the office for the last time was a low point, but also a fresh start. I hated what I was doing. Hated it. I didn't believe in the hair-growth pills or the metabolism boosters or the insurance conglomerates we were marketing. I originally believed the desire to go out on my own was because of the strained relationship with my brother, but I realized I didn't want to start a business in this area either. Recognizing I didn't like the work I had devoted thousands of hours to was difficult, but it wasn't right for me. I didn't know what I wanted to do with the rest of my life, but this wasn't it.

So I left my first genuine career, where I had learned to manage people, improve efficiencies, and make short-term sacrifices for long-term gains. As the company grew, I had also learned how to utilize software to make our team more productive without increasing overhead. We constantly developed new systems that saved our team hundreds of hours, so they were free to focus on revenue-building projects. This showed me that you could leverage technology to accomplish a lot with a little, whether money, people, or time.

Additionally, I realized there were opportunities to be successful even during hard economic times. We started the company in 2008, at the beginning of the recession, and were able to build, grow, and sell the business over the next three years. I continued to work for the company after the sale, my role grew from task doer to leader, and I became a go-between for the frontline workers who interacted directly with clients and those who preferred to keep their gaming headphones on at work and code. I watched my brother and his business partner sacrifice short-term financial gain to ensure future growth. When we could afford it, we invested in qualified and experienced team members who would be instrumental in our success for years to come. I discovered that a stubborn work ethic and getting people on board with your ideas is the way to reach goals and build an effective team. I may have grown to hate the work, but I couldn't deny that the job had provided me with invaluable experience.

When I arrived home that day, I was nervous to tell Shea about my last day in the office. Even though we'd discussed my plan to eventually strike out on my own, she wasn't prepared for my impulsive decision. On top of that, she had no idea I wanted to change industries as well. I walked in the door, sat on the bottom of our stairs, and told Shea, "I'm done." With little income and a California-sized mortgage, I had to find a solution to help pay our bills. I could feel the weight of my decision and was unsure how it would impact our future. Our freshly painted walls came crashing down around us, and I was lost.

Shea

Now it was my turn to be Syd's support system, carry us through this heavy time, and help him realize his talents and passion could be channeled into something beautiful. He'd been patient with me for years as I changed careers multiple times and let fear of failure guide me. I was his partner, and I would show up for him.

Syd's decision to search for a more fulfilling career altered the course of our entire lives. Pivotal moments that bring us to our knees mold us into the people we are today. I wasn't going to stand by and watch him make a hasty career move he'd later regret. He had made his decision, and I had made mine. I'd do whatever it took to help us ride out the next few months until he discovered what he was truly passionate about.

six

ADD LAYERS AND TEXTURE

*Incorporate rough and smooth forms
to build character in a space.*

Syd

The first thing I did was sell the servers. I posted them on Craigslist and hoped someone would take them off my hands. A week later I was sitting in a parking lot in Irvine, waiting for a stranger to show up so I could sell him the equipment out of the back of my car. On the way home I had to laugh at how shady the whole operation felt. I guess you could say I was burning the ships. I felt both liberated and scared. In my mind, selling the servers signaled that there was no going back to my old career.

I needed time to calm my mind, so I avoided the toll roads and took the scenic route. I had accepted the job from my brother during what I thought would just be a hiatus from college, but I ended up being really good at it. So good that I never returned to finish my degree. Was I just lucky that I'd stumbled into a profitable industry and my brother gave me a job? On one hand, yes.

But I had taken that luck and worked for the rest. It had been an incredible opportunity, but now what?

Finishing college would take years, and I didn't even like it. I had already decided that working for someone else wasn't for me. But I didn't have a business idea I felt passionate enough about to promote, and starting a business takes time and money, neither of which were on my side.

When I returned home, Shea had already entered into full-blown planner mode. "Okay, so I think we should go all in on my design business," she said.

Shea

Syd may not have known what he should do next, but I knew. I told him, "Syd, everything you're really good at is the exact opposite of what I'm good at. That makes us the perfect team. We complement each other so well—we should work together." However, Syd didn't see it that way.

I wasn't surprised when Syd left his brother's company, but I was caught off guard when he decided to change directions altogether. I wanted him to find something that made him light up the way I did with design, a pursuit that excited me to my core. I designed homes in my mind at breakfast, thought about tile while brushing my teeth, and walked the hallways of my clients' homes as I drifted to sleep. Over the next eight months Syd seemed to wander around in a wilderness, searching for the right fit, but nothing worked out. I wanted to give him as much time as he needed, but unfortunately, time wasn't something we had a lot of.

Syd

My timing for quitting my job and doing a complete career change couldn't have been worse. We had just sunk most of our savings into buying and remodeling our house. In the middle of the remodel we had a baby. Shea's business was growing, but it was still a start-up. Start-ups need time to breathe and develop. Small Business 101 says when you start a new business, you pour as much of your profit as possible back into the business to enable it to grow and reach its full potential. Now we needed to pull money out of the business to live.

We weren't living like rock stars, but paying our mortgage, utilities, insurance, and food added up. I took a few contract jobs here and there to help wherever possible, but it wasn't enough.

Shea

Watching Syd struggle was hard. He's always been a laid-back guy with a good dad joke up his sleeve and zero fear. But his zeal began to slip away. He doubted himself and became more withdrawn. Yet he wasn't the only one struggling. I was taking every project that came my way and doing my best to figure out how to be a new mom, run a business, and cheerlead for my husband.

In the mornings I would drive down to the beach with Wren and walk with her in the jogger stroller. She had reflux and was a fussy baby, but when we stepped onto the trail, she'd settle down and crane her neck as far as she could to put her ear closer to the sound of the waves. I didn't listen to music during these walks so I could quiet my mind and tell myself it was all going to be okay. By the end of the trail I was ready to conquer another day.

But then I'd pull into the driveway and go upstairs to our office, and I would immediately begin to feel the defeat.

Syd never again wanted to roll out of bed and see a desk, so we decided to share my office space in our nine-by-nine upstairs spare bedroom. It was painted charcoal gray and had two desks that faced opposite walls. It was so tight we took turns getting out of our chairs to avoid hitting each other. A glass door led out to the Juliet balcony above our garage, with white built-ins flanking either side. Our desks were a washed wood with a rough top, which Syd hated because it made his handwriting wobbly. I placed a framed navy blue constellation chart on his side and a linen pinboard above my desk. I filled it with images from J.Crew catalogs, design magazines, swatches, and drawings. Wren was a few months old, and I'd bring toys in for her to play with, but she preferred to roll around, chew on fabric samples, and bang on the printer.

At that point, the majority of my business was a roster of one-room projects. I'd juggle about fifteen of these small projects at a time. About ten of them would be at homes nearby and the rest were what I called e-designs. Many of my Instagram followers weren't local, so I cast a wider net for potential clients and offered to do furniture and decor selections remotely, for a fixed rate. The service included a design board, space plan, and shopping list. The turnaround time was quick because clients implemented my suggestions on their own.

But they weren't quick enough. Our savings account was empty because we'd spent our money on redoing our house. If I'd known Syd was going to quit his job as soon as we finished, we never would have started. We wouldn't have even purchased the house in the first place, but none of that mattered now.

Syd

We canceled cable. We canceled gym memberships. We stopped going out to eat. We cut out everything that wasn't mortgage or food, and even with that we had a strict grocery budget. I started selling off my bikes and surfboards and anything else I thought we could live without to give us a little breathing room. I sold a table we kept in the garage and a sofa I didn't think we needed anymore. It came down to the question: Could we live without it? If we could, we sold it.

But no matter how much we cut our expenses, something always came up. We started using the credit card for emergencies, which turned into using the credit card for anything we couldn't cover at the end of the month. We were losing ground quickly, making my lack of contribution even worse.

After Shea walked the beach trail every morning, she spent every other moment tending to Wren or her business. The sound of Wren giggling as Shea blew raspberries on Wren's chubby belly almost physically hurt because I knew that minutes later Shea would have to shift her attention away from their precious time together to keep up with her design projects. I'd hang with Wren while Shea met with clients, but she was always juggling phone calls during nap time, Instagram posts while Wren jumped in the bouncer, and e-designs until all hours of the night.

Shea

A few months earlier I'd never had to think about what I bought at the grocery store. Now I stood in the middle of the cereal aisle, comparing the prices of generic brands before I put one in my cart. My cheeks would flush as the cashier rang me up. More than once I had to put things back to get the total under our weekly budget. The worst weeks were when I had to pay for groceries with a credit card.

I was angry at myself for failing to provide basic necessities for my family. I was ashamed that I cared what other people would think. I felt sick knowing we would have a safety net if I hadn't been so focused on spending all our money to build my portfolio.

I wanted to support Syd, but some days I felt like too much was placed on my shoulders. I began to feel resentful he'd put us in this position. I was frustrated when I drove by moms at the park in the middle of the day, while I toted my baby to an upholstery shop. There was guilt when I checked emails while feeding her cereal puffs and sadness when I sat in her room and rocked her.

Wren's room, with the hummingbird wallpaper and sheepskin rug, was my escape. I could shut the door, rest my head on the back of the glider, and let the tears fall. I'm a fighter, but I couldn't see my way out of this situation. I examined our circumstances a million different ways. We could take out a loan to fund my business and go into even more debt, ride out the storm and hope Syd figured out what he wanted to do with his life, take on more projects to fill the few hours I had left in the day, or sell our house and move back into an apartment. All our choices felt either unsustainable or like giving up.

The lowest point came when Wren turned one. I wanted to buy her a birthday dress, doll her up, and for just one day pretend like everything was okay. I called my mom and wept on the phone. "I just want to make my little girl's birthday special," I sobbed. We couldn't afford a dress, and we really couldn't afford to buy her any presents. By this point we regularly had to use credit cards to pay for groceries and everything else we needed to live. I could have charged a dress too, but that wasn't the point. The point was that my daughter was turning one and we didn't have money to do anything for her.

"Oh, my girl," my mom said. "You are strong, and you'll get through this."

A couple of days later, a box showed up on our doorstep. Inside was a blue-and-white gingham dress with pink smocking around the neck and matching bloomers. I put a huge, white grosgrain bow around Wren's round head and pulled on her party dress as she tried to alligator roll away from me. We barbecued and sang "Happy Birthday" while Wren clapped, but an underlying sense of anxiety lingered in the air.

Syd

I hated putting us in this position and regretted leaving my job without a promising next step. I explored taking the test to get my real estate license and dabbled in web development. I built a few sites for local mortgage lenders, pest control companies, and an upcoming marathon. I should have determined what I was going to do before making a rash decision.

All the while, bills kept showing up, and we were falling further and further behind. I hate debt, but we now had nearly $20,000 in credit card bills and no end in sight. We had no way of paying it down. Most months we paid the minimum payment.

I knew something had to change.

One day Shea was feeling particularly overwhelmed from

dealing with a huge remodel about an hour away from our house, managing her other projects, and tending to Wren as she fussed. "If you have nothing else to do right now, can you at least help me organize these invoices I have to send out?" she asked me. I told her, "Sure, anything."

When I sat down in front of her computer, I couldn't believe my eyes. Shea had saved everything she'd ever done onto her Mac desktop—every photograph, every invoice, every order form, and every document. Because no room was left on the screen, the files had started to form layers.

"What is all of this?" I asked. "Your desktop is a mess."

Shea shot me a look. "I'm doing the best I can."

I didn't say anything else. Instead, I started moving files off the desktop and into folders. I found the invoices she needed and sent them out.

Over the next few weeks, I kept helping Shea like this until it became routine. Shea is an artist. She can walk into a room and see beauty where nothing beautiful yet exists. God has given her a natural talent, but running a design business requires a lot more than creating beautiful, livable spaces. The more time she had to spend on the nuts and bolts of the business, the less time she had to do the work that made the business grow. Someone needed to take that burden off of her shoulders. I thought that someone might as well be me until I could figure out what I was doing with my life.

Shea

The more Syd helped me behind the scenes, the more I kept at him, telling him we needed to do this together. I spent months saying, "We could do this, Syd. We could really do this." He knew business. I knew design. It made perfect sense to me, but Syd was reluctant. His response was always the same: "I will never work with family again." But I wasn't just family—I was his wife. And I was convinced we'd make a great team. While I loved creating beautiful spaces for people, I had no idea what it meant to streamline processes or improve efficiency. At the time, he viewed his contributions as working *for* me instead of *with* me. With no other plans at the moment, Syd agreed to help me . . . secretly.

Syd

Organizing Shea's desktop was the least of things I needed to get in order. How in the world she ever got anything done is beyond me. For instance, I'd ask, "So what's the system I use for ordering custom furniture?"

Shea would proceed to outline an archaic ten-step process, followed by, "And then you fax it over."

"You're kidding, right? Fax it over?" I asked. This was when I figured out that the interior design industry wasn't just a few years behind, but decades. Many of those kinds of companies still operated on a paper system, and, per the usual, Shea was just following the rules.

My nature is to do the exact opposite, so I started searching for work-arounds. I'd sweet-talk sales reps into letting me pay invoices with a credit card instead of mailing them checks. I edited Shea's website so the inquiry form gave us more information to filter projects before she spent time on the phone. I asked Shea to make a list of every non–design-related task she was doing and transferred each of those items from her plate to mine. Shea would spin her desk chair around and tease me with her elbow, saying, "See, we make a great team!"

As for me, I was shifting into start-up mode again.

Shea

Wren had reflux, which was exhausting, but she was always a good sleeper. Syd and I would use early mornings to check our emails and tiptoe around the house until the bird woke up. We'd whisper to each other about our schedule for the day, joke about how many faxes needed to be sent, and for the first time in months, work became fun. I spent a lot of time looking at real estate listings in the mornings to see if I could find a less expensive home in our neighborhood, but was discouraged to find that home prices had risen far above what Syd and I paid for our short sale.

My parents had recently moved from Texas to Utah and were building a home in a small farming community outside of Park City. Like Syd and me, my parents had met in Provo, Utah. My dad was from North Carolina and my mom was from Eugene, Oregon. The son of a tobacco farmer and the daughter of an astrophysicist, they graduated and followed my dad's FBI assignment to the Houston, Texas, office. While I was growing up, they always talked about their dream to leave the heat and return to Utah, where they could be surrounded by the mountains and feel all four seasons.

After saying goodbye to my childhood home and living there for twenty years, my mother was ecstatic to build the house they'd retire in. Building is a lengthy process, so my parents moved nearby to keep an eye on the progress. My mom enlisted me to design the finishes throughout, and we constantly chatted on the phone about tile and faucets. We shared Pinterest boards and texted each other images that inspired us. An appreciation for personal style and design has always been a shared interest of ours, and the project was a welcome distraction.

Also, this was my first opportunity to select every finish throughout an entire home and my first "client" who trusted my advice implicitly. Early in my business, clients hired me from what they could see in my limited portfolio and because I was charging half the going rate. I'd share my opinions, but the rapport wasn't built yet, and I was often asked to incorporate pieces and ideas that weren't a full representation of my design point of view. My mom and I were on the same page, and this was my chance to be part of a new home build with stylistic free reign.

We road-tripped to Utah a few times to check on the progress of my parents' home, and I was jealous of how much house you could get for the money. Our business was developing, and Syd and I were both feeling optimistic about the future of Shea McGee Design. But our bare-minimum overhead was so high in Orange County that it felt like we could survive but never get ahead.

My parents' move and the slower pace of life inspired me. Their new environment had less traffic, a plethora of outdoor activities, and more space. From gas to groceries, everything was less expensive. We had even started to receive design requests from potential clients in the area.

I hinted to Syd that we should consider moving to Utah. I told him that house prices in Orange County were skyrocketing again, and because we had remodeled our home, we'd make enough money to pay off our debt, fund the start of our business, and still have savings left over. I wasn't even sure if it was true, but it felt good to say the remodel I pushed us into might pay dividends.

However, I wanted to give him space to make the decision on his own. So I only asked him every day for four months.

Syd

I didn't bite, but I also didn't shoot down the idea. For a kid who grew up on the beach, moving to a landlocked state with snow sounded like one of the worst things I could do. Why would anyone want to leave the beach to go shovel snow? But as the weeks passed and we went deeper and deeper into the hole, I started to think it wasn't such a bad idea.

I didn't tell Shea this at the time, but I thought maybe she was onto something. Maybe we needed to make a drastic change to give us a fresh start and a renewed perspective.

I loved working with Shea because we saw eye to eye on most things. She was happy she didn't have to send invoices anymore, and we balanced each other's strengths. We were in the trenches and it was tough, but sharing the burden and a common goal heartened us.

The more I was immersed in the design industry, the more holes I saw. And holes meant opportunities for Shea and me to make our mark. It made a lot of sense, and if we combined forces we could do more than survive. I finally saw what Shea had seen all along: we could run a business together and build a brand no one had seen before.

Shea

We uttered many prayers as a couple that year. We'd start with gratitude. We were grateful for our health and our sweet baby girl. Then we'd quickly move to, "What should we do? Please guide us." We were waiting for a "lightning strike" moment, but it never came.

One morning, instead of tiptoeing over to the bathroom to brush his teeth like usual, Syd sat straight up in bed and said, "I think we should move to Utah. Let's do this." I never thought my Southern California boy would leave, but I knew in my heart he was right.

The next thing out of his mouth was, "But we have to change the name."

Shea McGee Design was a solo act, and we were a team now. We both felt that if we were going to do something, we were going to do it big. Syd may have hesitated at first, but once he was in, he was all in. But now we needed a name.

On Sundays we'd cruise around and admire the newly built homes in Newport Beach. A half-mile stretch between Avocado and Hazel Avenues is called the flower streets, with names like Carnation, Dahlia, and Poppy. The area was established in the 1950s with one-story bungalows nestled in neat rows. Over the last few decades, many of the homes had been leveled to make room for towering multimillion-dollar homes with nonexistent backyards, all clamoring for a view of the ocean on their rooftop decks. The city's best architects and designers created many of the homes, and we loved to drive by, take notes, and be inspired while strategizing our company's future.

That Sunday my notes were about brainstorming names for our business. We toyed with McGee Designs, McGee Home,

McGee Studio, McGee Interiors—every combination of the name McGee paired with an interior design term went on the list. We couldn't agree on *the one*, so we drove around while Wren napped and we talked about our ideas for the future.

Syd

In our car, in the office, and at the dinner table, Shea and I had many conversations about the direction of our new company, including a lot of back and forth regarding exactly what our roles were going to be. It wasn't as simple as Shea doing the creative side and me doing the business side. I'm creative in my own way, and Shea's communications background helped with the business. This division of responsibility ultimately took a couple of years to sift through.

Once we gave ourselves permission to go all in, it became clear we both had big dreams. During one of the first conversations we had, I told Shea that design work by itself wasn't scalable, so to grow, we needed a product to sell. "Other designers have product lines," I said. "We need to get in on that." Did we have any idea how to make that happen? Of course not, but that didn't stop us.

Shea

I was already working long hours to keep up with our clients and agreed that selling products would be a natural complement to the business. Did that mean doing online sales, having a physical brick-and-mortar store, or both? We didn't know. Maybe yes to all. Syd had a vision for expanding far beyond what I was already doing, but I wasn't sure what that would look like.

"I could design fabrics and we could sell pillows," I told Syd. "People buy them in multiples, and they don't break in shipping." The problem was, I still couldn't draw, so I couldn't translate the ideas in my head into something tangible.

We had a large fiddle-leaf fig tree planted in a seagrass basket right next to the French doors in our kitchen nook. I babied that tree with ten ounces of water every six days. The leaves were large and glossy, and it was lopsided, as the branches on one side stretched to feel the sun. Our tree continued to grow even when we were falling short, and it was my inspiration for our first textile.

Syd

Our neighbor, one of my best friends, was a creative director for one of the big surf brands. He had taught me some Adobe Illustrator basics, so I plucked off one of our tree's leaves, traced the fig-leaf pattern, and scanned it into the computer. The trick was not getting a single fig leaf on the screen but creating a pattern that still looked good when you printed out eight hundred yards of it.

Shea sat next to me as I tried to create the pattern. "Try desaturating it," she said. "Can you at least rotate it?"

"I don't know how to do that," I kept saying over and over. My Illustrator skills left a lot to be desired.

Once we got it close, my buddy cleaned it up for us and helped us put it in a proper repeat so it was prepared for printing. We borrowed his Pantone swatches and saved the files because we still needed to find a printer and come up with the money to buy the raw fabric yardage. We would've preferred to have someone do the entire design, but we couldn't afford that.

A few days after our drive through the flower streets, I jokingly referred to our spare bedroom office as "the studio" to make it sound fancy. The closet never fully closed because fabric samples were falling out of the baskets, fiddle-leaf fig leaves withered on our desks, the printer sat on the floor, and Wren happily pushed buttons on anything her tiny hands could reach. At that moment Shea said, "That's it!" And from that spare bedroom-turned-office, Studio McGee was born.

And by the way, that fig-leaf pattern became one of our bestsellers over the next couple of years.

Shea

Once we had a name that represented the two of us, we knew it was time to make the move. I had one wish before leaving, and that was to take family photos in our home. I hired a photographer to come over and asked her to shoot a few posed photos, but mostly I wanted her to capture candid shots of our family in our element in our first home together.

Wren was wiggly and happily let us chase her as she crawled all over the house, reaching for the driftwood on the coffee table and patting her hand on the cold marble. All our homes have been filled with layers and textures, some smooth and others rough, and they work together to tell the story of who we are. We smiled not because there was a camera nearby but because for the first time in a long time, we felt the peace that comes from knowing you're doing what you were made for.

After the photo shoot, we listed our home, and it sold within a few days. Three weeks later, we loaded up the moving truck and were ready to relocate to Utah.

seven

START WITH A CLEAN SLATE

*Clear the clutter so you have room to
see the potential in front of you.*

Syd

Relocating to Utah was our "push the chips to the middle of the table," all-in move. Shea and I wanted to change the lens through which the world viewed design and build an empire.

In my mind, designers maintained a longstanding reputation of snobbery—the title alone made me think of a woman toting a small dog in her purse, saying "vahz" instead of vase. We believed we could help people see it was possible for good design to feel both beautiful and approachable.

The two of us joked about the "build an empire" part, but deep down we both meant it. If we believed in ourselves enough to take a risk like this, why would we aim small? We channeled our energy from survival to setting our sights as high as we could aim.

The shift in our perspective was drastic. We went from spending all of our energy to keep everything in our possession to figuring out what other sacrifices could be made to reach our goals. If that meant selling our house to raise capital and moving to Utah to minimize expenses, we were in. As much as I loved living near the beach, I had much bigger aspirations.

Shea

I never thought Syd would leave the beach, but once he said we should move, there was no second-guessing his commitment. We were ready. I have never felt so certain of a decision in my entire life. I believed we were inspired to move and had faith the pieces would fall into place as they were intended. Moving would give us a clean slate so we could clearly see the potential in front of us.

Other than our parents, we had told few people we were working together. I was saving that announcement for a classic designer reveal, when I'd say goodbye to Shea McGee Design and hello to Studio McGee!

My old logo was a scripted font with a leafy laurel wreath underneath. Syd was not on board with using my dainty logo, so before we moved we began to search for new logo inspiration. We would look separately, bring our ideas together, and try to find the common threads. Syd's skills in Illustrator had improved (slightly) since he drew our first textile pattern, so we decided to create a new logo on our own to save money.

When we entered our brand-concept meeting at the kitchen table, surrounded by moving boxes, we happily discovered our inspirations were similar. The logos were simple, with all caps and no icons or flourishes. While I sat next to Syd with Wren in my lap, he'd toy around with various serif and sans serif typefaces, and

I'd give a thumbs-up or thumbs-down. We eventually settled on Century Gothic, in all caps, with a black-and-white color palette.

"We need a tagline," I said. "People need to know what we're all about." I didn't want to force it and come up with something on the spot, so I continued to mull it over as we packed and prepared to launch our new website.

The way we positioned our announcement on Instagram was critical. I wanted to share with our community of thirty thousand followers that we were taking a leap and moving to another state, and that Syd and I were going into business together. I wanted them to be part of our entrepreneurial journey, and the announcement was an important first step in convincing people to take us seriously.

A few days before we loaded the moving truck, I received our family photos from our photographer. In one picture all of us were on the sofa and Syd was lifting Wren into the air. My hand was on his back while we both laughed, trying to get Wren to smile. We were in the center, but the photographer had pulled back far enough that you could see the living room on either side, the kitchen behind us, and the fiddle-leaf fig tree, with its large green leaves, peeking out from the nook. She had managed to capture both our design perspective and the spirit of our family in a single moment. This would be our announcement picture.

Even with turbulence behind us and uncertainty ahead of us, Syd and I were determined to use our experience and channel it into something magnificent. We had allowed ourselves the space to feel let down, allotted time for reality to sink in, and mourned the disappointments. But we also had known there was opportunity if we chose to look for it.

The day before the move, as I lay next to Wren on a blanket

spread out on our bare wood floor, it came to me. *Make life beautiful*. Regardless of our circumstances, we'd choose to see the good. Beauty wasn't just about marble countertops and fresh flowers, although those things are quite lovely. Our mantra was also about making a conscious decision to find strength from our journey.

Syd

Part of my journey meant overcoming my ego. I was self-conscious when family members said, "Oh, are you working *for* Shea now?" The low jabs hit me right where I was most vulnerable. Instead of brushing off their comments, I'd question everything—the move, the business, all of it. Part of me wondered if people would view our partnership as a default decision because I'd failed to develop my own ideas. I hate that I cared about their opinions, but I did.

As much as I could, I made peace with the decision through logic: The company was already profitable but had plenty of opportunity for growth. People were drawn to Shea's style, and in the short time we'd worked together, we'd made huge strides that would have been impossible alone. This wasn't our only choice, yet it was the right choice for us.

I was either going to let the haters bother me or get over it. I decided to get over it and start building something. I chose to reframe my mindset. Shea and I were partners in life and in business. As partners, we had to trust that each of us would carry our weight. Shea managed anything visual, like client work, product design, marketing, photography, and Instagram. I took responsibility for new business, accounting, production, and technology.

Clarity of direction and purpose imparted a certain grit I'd lacked the previous year. I was more decisive and innovative as I shaped my role as a cofounder and the CEO of Studio McGee. CEO was a very self-confident title for a company of two without a real balance sheet. But I think I was more nervous about changing to a Utah driver's license than I was about getting Studio McGee off the ground.

Shea

I was so excited about launching Studio McGee. But when our house sold in less than three weeks, I realized I wasn't ready to walk away from this place where I'd invested so much of myself. However, we couldn't stay here and achieve our dreams with the business. We'd cut our budget as low as we could, and we'd sold off so much that we had little to load into the moving truck. Syd had even sold his Toyota truck, which he used to haul his surfboards back and forth to the beach. When he handed over the keys, I knew he was serious. Syd loved that truck.

On the day of the move, after Syd threw the last few things into the moving truck, I took a final walk through the house. I climbed up the stairs and headed toward Wren's nursery. As soon as I reached the top of the stairs I had to laugh at the paint line that ran along the baseboards. I thought about the thick, brown shag carpeting and all the Legos that had stabbed our feet.

And then I walked into Wren's room. The mint green wallpaper with hummingbirds stared back at me. The room had been . . . perfect. I once again thought about how, over the past few months, as money got tight and my stress heightened, this room had been my refuge, my place to rock Wren to sleep and block it all out. The glider was now in the trailer, along with the vintage gold leaf mirror, Wren's white crib, and every piece of furniture I'd meticulously selected. Everything was gone but the paint and wallpaper.

I thought about how excited I'd been with each step of designing and decorating this space. In a way, this room had made Studio McGee possible, because the photos of it that I'd posted on Pinterest and Instagram blew up beyond anything I could have predicted. This nursery wasn't just a room. It was everything to me.

Then it hit me—this room was now someone else's room to repaint and redecorate. I stared at the hummingbirds. *They'll probably be gone soon*, I thought. Everything that had made this space so special would soon be nothing but a memory.

I sat down in the middle of the room, hugged my knees to my chest, and sobbed. We were doing the right thing, but that didn't make it any easier to walk away from a place I loved.

Syd

As we drove away that day, looking back at our house in the rearview mirror felt like a scene from a movie. Neither Shea nor I could believe it was really happening. It had taken us months to find that house. We'd made offers on so many homes, only to have someone else swoop in at the last minute and outbid us. Finding that house was a gift. When we'd moved in, we both expected it would be our forever home. Forever lasted all of two years. However, we had money in the bank, zero debt, and a runway for our start-up. For a while we could live on the money we made off the house and pour all our profits back into the business. We had a plan, and now we had the liquidity to work the plan.

As much as we loved that house, we planned to buy something much cheaper in Salt Lake City. We figured we might as well make payments toward a mortgage and use the home for content instead of paying rent. We wanted to find an inexpensive house that needed updates but was in good enough condition that we could live in it while renovating. Shea planned to share each step of the journey, which would both keep her audience engaged and expand our portfolio in a new market. This marketing strategy had already worked once, and we were certain it would work again in Utah, even if on a smaller scale.

Unfortunately, the mortgage companies had a different idea. When we applied for a loan, everyone turned us down. Shea and I were both officially self-employed. To qualify for a mortgage, we had to show two years of income from the same business. Studio McGee was a brand-new LLC with zero track record. Everywhere we went, we heard the same thing: "We're sorry. You don't qualify for a mortgage. Come back and talk to us in a couple years."

Shea

When all the banks turned us down for a loan, I didn't know what we'd do. Finding a place to live wasn't the problem, because we could always rent. The problem was that I wouldn't have a place where I could showcase my design point of view. Much of our marketing strategy was built around sharing our personal home transformations, and I wasn't sure how we'd get people to trust me as a designer when we couldn't use our home as a reflection of our business. It was a huge setback, and we needed to come up with a plan B.

Before we moved, Syd and I had talked a lot about where we needed to focus our attention to reap the biggest return on our investment. I loved designing spaces for clients, but to scale the overall business to the level we hoped to achieve, we needed to grow the product side. Now that we couldn't use our own home remodel as a marketing tool, perhaps we needed to dive into our retail ideas.

Syd was already developing our first website and working on the online store. We were still in the process of finalizing exactly how to manufacture textiles, but our game plan was to exclusively sell pillows until we could expand the shop and build it into an e-commerce brand that sold furniture, lighting, rugs, and decor. The Las Vegas Market was coming up, and we were only four hundred miles away.

Syd

If you have no idea what Market is, you know how I felt before I went to our first one. When I started setting up accounts with different product vendors and meeting with reps for designer companies, they'd always say something like, "Will I see you at Market this year?" I didn't know what they were talking about, but I'd reply, "Sure. Yeah. Definitely." I finally googled the Las Vegas Market and discovered it's a design trade show that happens twice a year, and you need a badge to enter. Buyers, brands, and designers travel from all over the country to see Vegas World

Market Center, which had become an all-inclusive furniture, gift, and home decor market featuring thousands of products.

Shea

We registered online a few weeks before attending Las Vegas Market using the business card and logo we'd designed ourselves. I felt very official walking in with a badge, but was soon overwhelmed by the number of showrooms to navigate and products to explore. Market is not a curated shopping experience; it is composed of three buildings, with about sixteen floors each, brimming with gifts, furniture, and decor. Think of every gift shop, boutique, and furniture store in America. Where do you think they buy the Poo-Pourri, overstuffed recliners, and Elf on the Shelf kits? They buy them at Market.

It was my job to sift through the clutter and curate pieces into a cohesive collection representing our style. My thrifting experience kicked in, and I started looking at every display to choose the perfect pieces to sell in our online store.

When we finally walked into a space filled with the most gorgeous light fixtures suspended in a canopy across a two-thousand-square-foot showroom, Syd and I were delighted to finally find a brand that resonated with our aesthetic. The shapes were substantial in scale, the brass was perfectly aged, and I was already using their pieces in quite a few upcoming client projects. I knew they would be a great fit for our store.

Their reaction, and every other meeting that day, was the same. They'd greet us with a smile. I'd introduce us: "We're Syd and Shea McGee of Studio McGee. We have a very engaged following on Instagram and are launching an e-commerce platform. We'd love to talk to you about carrying your products."

"Uh, Instagram? I think my daughter told me about that," we heard over and over. This was the summer of 2014. Social media wasn't new, but it was to the design industry. "Where'd you say your store is?"

"We don't have a brick-and-mortar store. We'll be doing all of our sales online," I'd reply.

The smiles that greeted us faded. "No, we only let people sell our products in real stores."

Not everyone shot us down exactly like this. A handful of vendors were willing to consider letting us carry their products, but only if we did a minimum order of $10,000 or more. Syd and I felt confident we'd arrive there someday, but that wasn't the day. We couldn't sink ten grand into one vendor out of the potential hundreds of vendors we wanted to put in our online store.

This experience was worse than being told no. Everyone treated us like we were nothing but a couple of kids pretending to be something we were not. Which was exactly what we were doing, but that was beside the point.

They didn't come out and say it, but their faces said, "Who let you sneak in here?" I was hurt. And Syd got mad.

Syd

I wasn't mad. I was pissed. When we got in the car to road-trip home from Vegas, Shea was upset. "What are we going to do now?" she asked. I didn't have a plan, but we weren't going to roll over and give up.

"I don't know, Shea," I answered, "but I do know we're going to prove them all wrong." This became the first step in the stages of Studio McGee grief, because it wasn't the last time we had a door slammed in our face. We'd get our hearts set on something only to be told, "No, you can't do that" by the gatekeeper. Next we'd feel upset and wonder what to do. Then we'd fire up and develop an "I'll show them" attitude. We were going to establish a reputation that made it impossible for vendors to say no to us.

We moved through the first few stages of grief quickly, but we realized proving the naysayers wrong could take months or possibly years. We also knew that every time something hadn't gone as expected, we would look back later and be relieved that things hadn't worked out the way we first planned.

We decided to proceed with producing our own pillows and place more emphasis on scaling the design business. We started with the fig-leaf textile and a few other prints we'd designed before leaving California. I had spent a day driving around LA's garment district and found a place that would print our fabric for us. However, the cost for the first run, including all initial set-up costs, would be $25,000. Then we needed to order about $3,000 in zippers. And of course, Shea didn't just want any zippers—she wanted gold ones.

We had barely pulled ourselves out of debt, and this was a lot of money. Our estimation was that we needed to live off of savings for a year and put all our earnings back into the business. If the pillows were a flop and we burned through our cash too fast, we would have nothing of value to sell and would have to move in with Shea's parents. We could be conservative, focus purely on building the design side of the business, and push the idea of an online store to the distant future. Or we could once again shove the chips to the center of the table and go for it. We went for it.

I created a shop page on our portfolio website, had the fabric printed in LA, and commissioned the pillows to be sewn locally. I kept a stack of boxes and a tape gun in our garage and would back out the car to make room for my shipping station. Most designers wait until they have an established career and reputation to launch their product lines. We may have followed the exact opposite method of how we should have started a Studio McGee product line, but orders started coming in, and it worked. We had no choice but to make it work.

A few months after Vegas Market, Shea flew out to North Carolina for another huge design trade show in High Point. We were shot down there as well. Over and over again. But the online store, product lines, and everything thereafter never would have happened if we hadn't put our heads down, worked hard, and prepared for things to start falling into place.

Shea

Getting shot down at both markets propelled me to be even more determined as a designer. I wanted the old guards in the industry to take me seriously. Each successful project brought new projects, usually of a higher caliber than the previous one. Syd and I took on as much work as we could to fast-track the growth of our business. I couldn't handle the workload alone, so we needed to hire a design assistant or two. I'd share my knowledge and cultivate their taste to align with our brand, and they'd help with the technical skills, like AutoCAD. My two years in design school taught me the basics of those programs, but I was slow and more interested in directing the design aesthetics. We needed to hire people who could do what I couldn't, and I'd teach them the rest.

The first weekend we lived in Salt Lake City, we interviewed to hire an assistant. Even before we'd packed our belongings in the moving truck, I shared a job posting on Instagram. I asked those interested to apply through our website and to attach a design board. A handful of people applied. I sorted through emails and reviewed the attachments. None of the applicants matched our style until I came across one design board that showed a dining room with a Saarinen tulip table paired with a jute rug, a traditional lantern, and faux bamboo chairs. A ceramic vase was placed on the table with wild greenery. Whoever this Carly was, she got it. I could see that her taste was aligned with ours and hoped she was a personality fit. "This is our first hire," I told Syd.

We arranged to meet Carly for lunch at Blue Plate Diner in East Salt Lake for an interview. From the moment we sat on the chrome and vinyl chairs, surrounded by old Elvis Presley posters and classic rock memorabilia, we clicked. Cat Stevens was blasting from the jukebox, and we had to yell throughout the interview, but no one seemed to mind because we felt like we'd known each other for years.

Carly had graduated from design school and apprenticed under another designer for about a year. She had a quiet confidence about her and seemed kind. And she was eager.

As the server placed the check on the table, I looked at Syd, then said to her, "You've got the job. Can you start on Monday?"

Thankfully, Carly accepted the job, even though we could only pay an hourly wage and didn't have an office. She came to our house and worked at our dining room table while Wren napped upstairs. She had never managed client work before, but she strove to learn as much as she could in a condensed time-frame. Training that should have taken her years to complete only took a few months.

Syd

Three people crowded around one small table, whispering to each other while a sound machine hummed upstairs, wasn't in our long-range business plan. But starting somewhere was better than waiting for perfect conditions. It's like surfing. You fall into one of two categories: you either check the weather and wait until the winds and swell are just right, or you paddle out regardless of the weather, happy to be in the ocean. Even if the water is choppy, you eventually catch something that you would have otherwise missed.

Shea and I weren't interested in standing on the shore, so we kept paddling at the kitchen table until we found our first office space. It was dilapidated, but we scrubbed the walls clean, slathered them in white paint, and gave ourselves a blank canvas so we could see the potential—both literal and figurative—ahead of us.

eight

LOOK FOR NATURAL LIGHT

| *Open your windows and feel the sunshine.* |

Shea

Syd and I spent hours combing through Craigslist, looking for office space, and the listings in our price range were slim. Our options were either abandoned insurance offices that hadn't been updated since the eighties, with marled burgundy carpet, an oak chair rail, and an acoustic tile ceiling, or windowless basements clearly not zoned for occupancy.

One day Syd came across a two-hundred-square-foot downtown loft space marketed as a photographer's studio. One block away from the PR firm I worked for my first year after college graduation, Pierpont Avenue was a street developed in the early 1900s that had been converted from a produce market to artist workspaces in recent years. There was an antique shop next door to the loft space and a jewelry workshop downstairs. The jewelry company owner was looking to sublease the top floor, and the asking rent was $800. She offered to throw in the room next door for an extra $200.

When we pulled onto Pierpont, I looked at Syd and said, "Well, it's not the worst place we've seen." He replied, "No, but it's close." I told him we should at least look inside before we crossed it off our list. I pulled Wren out of her car seat, and Syd shouted over the car not to let her out of my arms. I looked down and saw used syringes scattered across the sidewalk.

We asked the woman showing us the building if that was the norm. She said, "See that park down the street? They have a 'knock it off' policy. The cops look the other way when people do drugs because it's easier to confine the misdeeds to the park than to arrest them."

"Let's just give it a chance," I said.

Syd looked down and shook his head.

Upstairs, I saw potential. The space was one open room with a wall of huge windows, wood rafters on the fifteen-foot ceiling, and exposed red brick walls.

"The ceiling looks like it's molding in areas," Syd replied.

The landlord spoke up. "Oh, those are char marks. The roof caught on fire a few years ago, but it's fine now."

"We can paint it," I said. To my optimistic eyes, the room was only a few steps away from being an industrial urban loft.

Syd opened the bathroom door to find years of grime and a smell to match. "Don't go in there."

We were willing to overlook the state of the bathroom because this place was the first one we'd toured with an ounce of a coolness factor and the right price. Syd hesitated, but after a few more weeks of searching and realizing that working at the kitchen table during nap time was slowing our momentum, we both knew the loft was our best option. We never signed a lease and paid in cash each month.

Syd

I thought the space was terrible, but all Shea saw was a challenge. Before we moved in we painted everything white, top to bottom. I mean everything. The walls. The floor. The ceiling. The soot from the fire bled through the paint, but after three coats, we had a studio. Every surface reflected light from the large windows, and even I felt inspired.

Shea said that our budget makeover space needed some "jewelry," so she devised a plan to hang two rows of three brass pendant lights from the rafters. Each dome light measured twenty inches in diameter and together they cost as much as a month's rent, but the effect was transformative.

Our ability to mix high and low has served us well through the years, in both design strategies and business growth. The lights consumed most of our budget, so we furnished with white IKEA desks and bookshelves. An evening of assembly and a few curse words later, Shea and I added brass hardware to the drawer fronts to elevate their basic profile and tie into the pendant lights. The space next door became our conference room, even though the drywall didn't extend all the way to the ceiling and you could hear every conversation drifting over the walls.

When we finished the makeover, it was hard to imagine how the office ever felt dark. It was bright, airy, and a complete one-eighty from when we'd started. If you could look past the shoddy exterior and ignore the smell of pot wafting up from the antique store, you would see a room full of ambition and light.

Our room provided an artistic atmosphere to create, but it didn't make us eager to invite clients downtown for meetings. We scheduled most meetings on-site or in clients' homes. But overall, the new office did exactly what we needed it to do. And whenever someone did stop by the office, we prayed they didn't need to use the bathroom. That bathroom made truck stop bathrooms look like a luxury resort.

Our rent didn't cover building maintenance, so we cleaned the bathroom ourselves, and the other tenants were always stealing our paper towels. When the weather turned cold in late fall, we found out the building didn't have heat, and the rustic brick walls meant there was no insulation. The following summer we discovered that our freestanding air-conditioning unit in the corner could double as a hand dryer. We stayed there for a year, until we felt confident we could sustain a lease agreement written on paper.

Shea

The office felt large when we first moved in with our staff of Syd, our one employee, and me. That feeling didn't last. Within weeks of hiring our first employee, we hired a second. A few weeks later, we hired two interns. And by "hired," I mean that we paid them in school credit. Our desks were pushed together, with about two and a half feet left to walk around the studio perimeter.

Work rolled in faster than Syd and I ever imagined. Since our plan to market the business by documenting a home renovation failed, and we were living in a rental with turquoise chandeliers and a fire-engine red fireplace, our backup strategy was to build our portfolio with client work as quickly as possible.

When I first started using Instagram to market my business, I promised myself I'd post a minimum of one time each day. No breaks. No excuses. Instagram was an integral part of our chain of demand. The more beautiful content we produced, the more photos we posted. The more photos we posted, the more followers we gained on Instagram. More followers became more inquiries for design projects, which kept the chain moving. To keep growing our Instagram account, and therefore our business, we had to keep posting original content.

We may not have been able to implement our first strategy, but our "say yes to everything" approach was working. Also, my parents were still building their home that I had started helping my mom with when we were living in California, and the timing couldn't have been better.

My mom and I have an uncanny resemblance to each other; she's often mistaken for my sister. Our relationship stretches beyond mother-daughter formality, as we could spend hours chatting like girlfriends about everything from the pair of shoes we'd scored on sale to a new cookie recipe we're testing. "Did your new *House Beautiful* arrive yet?" she'd say. "I think the kitchen they featured is right up your alley."

Our mutual love of style and design shaped my taste from an early age and still influences my design perspective. Growing up we didn't have the means to hire designers, but my mom shared with me her love of classic, foundational pieces that could stand the test of time. She saved for years to purchase the sofa she admired: an English roll-arm with linen upholstery, turned legs, and brass casters. She had a knack for making her HomeGoods pillows look three times more valuable than what she paid for them.

When my mom had asked me to help design their home, I was definitely still an intern, working for portfolio credit, but my parents' trust gave me the opportunity to prove I was capable of designing an entire home. Their home became more than a project—it was critical to the future success of our business.

My dad's direction was to stay under budget and make room for his guitar, and my mom's direction was to keep the design one part coastal and one part traditional. "Do what you do best," she said. "I just want it to feel like a breath of fresh air when I walk into our home."

Syd

Shea's parents' house gave us exposure and also connected us with their young, eager contractor, Steve, who also had good design instincts. Like Shea, he was inspired by the charm of old houses—moldings and millwork, intimate spaces, and an updated take on traditional design. He not only built the house but also created the architectural plans himself, allowing Shea to be involved in the process. Instead of arguing with her on all the design choices, they collaborated. I think Steve recognized in us what we saw in him and realized that scoring a client with good taste early in our careers was a big break for us all.

Before we moved, Shea and I put thousands of miles on our car, driving back and forth between California and Utah to check on her parents' home. I would drop Shea off at the house, and she'd pull on her wellies and trudge through the snow, carrying her tote bag brimming with tile samples and a tape measure. "Call you in a few hours!" she'd yell back to the car.

I'd take Wren to wave at the cows in a nearby field while Shea and her mom ticked off their punch list. After Shea finished on-site, we'd trade off while I took a few phone calls, then I'd step into my role as Instagram husband, snapping a few pictures of Shea measuring things in the house, to post later and tag with #themidwayhouse.

Once we were in Utah and shared more photos of her parents' home, people began hiring Steve and Studio McGee as a team. We did a couple more projects together, and before long, each project was bigger than the previous one and we were all reaching a caliber of clientele we had only dreamed about. Every time we received a new client inquiry, I'd ask how they found us. "I saw a picture of a mudroom you designed, and then I clicked on the link and saw your Midway House," they'd say. "I want my house to feel just like that."

Shea

Of all the rooms I designed for my parents, their mudroom is probably the most copied room I've ever designed to this day. The room itself was an unusual feature in the home because it was situated between the kitchen and garage, with doors on both ends, like a breezeway leading from the front yard to the back. To maximize the square footage, Steve and I made this space the hardest-working room in the home. It fit a washer and dryer, a built-in bench with hooks, storage for cleaning supplies, and a powder bathroom in one corner. The mudroom was a landing zone to drop groceries and snowy boots, and a place for grandkids to run in from the backyard with muddy feet and wet swimsuits after playing in the sprinklers.

Although the space was utilitarian in nature, it would also be my parents' main entry on a daily basis, so I wanted it to feel special. Knowing my mom's desire for a coastal traditional home, I thought shiplap walls were the perfect solution to make the most of the long, narrow space. We coated the shiplap one of my favorite paint colors, Simply White by Benjamin Moore, and put down a tile floor for durability. Our budget was stretched, and I searched for a tile that was affordable while also making a statement. Like me, my mom loved natural stone materials that would never go out of style. Marble would stain, and porcelain fit the budget but lacked character. I needed an affordable stone tile with depth to hide dirt, and planned to lay it in a herringbone pattern for interest.

I couldn't find inspiration pictures of a floor like I had in mind, so I described my vision to Steve. He suggested we use a twelve-by-twelve slate because it cost less than three dollars a square foot, and then we'd ask the tile installer to cut it in half to achieve the herringbone pattern.

With all of the black and white in the space, I decided to add warmth by placing a butcher block countertop across the top of the washer and dryer as a place to fold laundry. We hung repeated pendants in a row to accentuate the hallway effect, a design element I've continued to use since.

When the home build was finished, my parents moved in with a mix of existing pieces and new furniture. I was in a rush to photograph the project and add it to our portfolio, but the designs were still missing some layers. So I incorporated furniture and accessories that we'd brought from California, to fill in the gaps and complete the spaces.

People want to feel the life and natural light in our work. An empty room doesn't draw you in like a full one. In a photograph you can take a room you designed, home in on vignettes, and create a mood. Like a home, a good portfolio image invites people into your world and makes them feel like they are there with you.

My number one rule for interior photography is to turn off all artificial light and open the shades as wide as possible. Emphasizing natural light allowed our spaces to feel fresher, more natural, and authentic. Syd and I often joked that the brighter the photo, the more likes it would get on Instagram.

I believe we all want to feel the sunshine, even if our lives are lacking it.

Syd

Shea's parents' home became a retreat for us. Our rental home was fine, but the owner loved pops of color and had put decorative knobs on every drawer, which snagged my pants. It was just under 1,500 square feet, with a combined kitchen, living, and dining space, and three bedrooms upstairs. The home's greatest asset was a large closet under the stairs, which opened into the living room. We hung twinkle lights from the sloped ceiling and the book ledges on the walls. Shea filled it with baskets of toys and turned it into a tiny playroom.

Our neighbors, however, were not fine. We lived in a suburb just south of Salt Lake City and landed on the one street in the entire city without children. I guess there was an unspoken rule (which the real estate agent "forgot" to mention) that it was a fifty-five-plus community. They hated us for disturbing the peace with sidewalk chalk and the sound of a child's laughter. We slipped into the garage every day for four years, so our neighbors wouldn't accost us with complaints about pink bicycles left on our lawn.

On Friday evenings we'd load up the car with the Pack 'n Play and drive an hour through Parley's Canyon just past Park City to the Millers' new home to camp out for the weekend. The drive was peaceful, and their house felt more like our home than our own did. The white kitchen reminded me of our house in California, with white marble countertops and a farmhouse sink facing the backyard. The rooms were intimate enough to feel cozy but spacious enough to gather as a family. We spent hours playing Bananagrams around the coffee table while Shea's parents spoiled Wren.

The Miller home had a vibe. Every single room had windows, and the sun hit every corner throughout the day. It felt easy and light. Like a weight was lifted the moment we walked in the door. Shea poured her heart into their home, and you could sense it. The design was so intentional that you could enjoy your surroundings without having to think about them.

Shea

We'd made one exception to the "say yes to everything" rule before we moved to Salt Lake City. I had a client in Southern California for whom I designed a couple of rooms in their home. Before we decided to move, they purchased acreage to build a high-end vacation home near Kamas, Utah. Nestled against national forest land and a short drive from Deer Valley Ski Resort, it was a quickly growing hot spot for luxury homes. They asked me to work on it for them, and after some thought, I said no. The home would be roughly nine thousand square feet, and I had never designed an entire house from the ground up. On top of that, Wren was a newborn, and I was overwhelmed with the demands of being a new mom. Also, this was when I still had the delusion that I'd take some time off from design to be home with Wren full-time.

These weren't the only reasons I said no. These clients planned to build a modern, multimillion-dollar estate. I didn't feel qualified to manage a project of that scale and was scared I would ruin the design. My portfolio was filled with transitional, coastal, and traditional-style homes; I wasn't sure I could design a modern home.

Ultimately, when I looked in the mirror, I still didn't see a real designer. Only a wannabe, someone with a few semesters of design classes at a school one step above a high school. Who was I to think I could take on a multimillion-dollar, modern mountain home and produce something beautiful?

"I can't," I told them.

"Can you at least look over the plans for us?" they asked. I told them I could do that and consulted for a few months, until they finalized their plans and awaited the permits.

After we moved to Salt Lake City, this same couple reached out again. They knew Syd and I had recently moved to start our business together, and I'm grateful they decided to ask one more time: "Are you sure you don't want to work on our house?"

I'd finished my parents' house, and the response was incredible. The images of my parents' home had already been reposted thousands of times. As a result, we were receiving inquiries for larger projects and building a team to support the growth. I also had Syd by my side, who said yes to everything.

I responded to my clients and said, "I'm so glad you reached out again! Yes, we'd love to work together on this project."

Syd

Shea's talent for designing homes was clear, but it was up to me to grow the business. Living off of savings while we were trying to build our business felt like flying the plane while trying to build it. I was operating from a place of scarcity, to not relive our past year.

While the design team worked in the studio, I'd often take calls in the conference room next door. As soon as I walked back into the room, they'd avoid making eye contact, knowing I was about to add another project to their plate. "It's a good one," I'd say. "I just couldn't say no."

My goal was to onboard new clients and then do whatever I could to give the designers the opportunity to do what they did best: design. I didn't want them bogged down with contracts, bills, orders, or pillow shipments. I managed all of the above, plus accounting and payroll. In the early days of our business, I also needed to build the framework for administrative needs we take for granted today: setting up LLCs and email accounts, Slack for messaging, processes for new hires, and ordering pepper spray for all of our employees.

My version of accounting was to bring in more than we spent. And my version of running payroll was filling out handwritten checks on a Friday as the team reminded me on their way out the door. Our first operational hire was a college senior studying accounting whose responsibilities included building financial models, making sure we didn't run out of money, and taking out the trash.

I continued to work with vendors to secure better discounts on products and spent days ordering hundreds of items for clients and facilitating the shipping and delivery. At one point I looked at my spreadsheets with dozens of open tabs and thought, *There has to be an easier way.* My past life directing the development of new technologies kicked in, and I started mapping the development of our own software. This would streamline the ordering process by categorizing each client by room, automating markups, and calculating shipping. There would be a place for clients to view the specified products and track orders.

This project took six months to launch but reduced my work-load by half. We hired an ordering specialist to take over this responsibility so I could focus on improving the software.

As we developed our ops team and made huge strides in our capacity for growth, our next step was to figure out how to scale the creative side of the business. Shea was good at design, but she was also really good at becoming a bottleneck to growth.

Shea

Maintaining high standards for myself and our team came easily to me, but letting go of responsibility did not. Establishing a productive creative relationship and building trust in one another take time. I needed to trust our designers' ability to represent our ideas without being micromanaged, and they had to trust me to lead our projects in the best visual direction for our clients and brand.

Our first year I worked side by side with our two lead designers, directing every inch of every drawing and attending every site visit so they could in turn train junior designers and interns to work alongside them. Their unrelenting work ethic and willingness to learn set an early standard for consistently beautiful work products.

The modern mountain home was one of the first projects we all collaborated on, and the square footage overwhelmed all of us. The home was a U-shape rambler built for entertaining. The center of the home was an open-concept kitchen, living room, and dining room, with vaulted ceilings and huge black windows above a sliding door system that extended across the entire back side of the house. The ceiling was an asymmetrical slope that started at twelve feet in the entry and rose to eighteen by the time you reached the back wall of windows. White oak beams spanned the entire length of the fifty-foot-long great room expanse. There were two master suites, multiple guest bedrooms, a bunk room, two laundry rooms, eight bathrooms, and a bonus room for ping-pong and pool.

Unrolling any plans for the first time, regardless of size, can be intimidating before you've fully immersed yourself in them. You have to take the lines on the paper and imagine how they'll be brought to life. Once we got past the initial shock, we could see that we'd designed that many rooms before—these just happened to be under one gorgeous, cedar-shingle roof.

Our clients were generous and kind, and they saw potential in me before I realized it in myself. They'd hired me, a budding designer, years prior, and now they were trusting me with a nicer home than I had ever stepped foot in until this point. Although part of me still believed I'd been handed an opportunity I didn't deserve, I was determined to take it and run with it. I wanted to pay back their trust with a home they could enjoy with their family for years to come. This project was to be my pièce de résistance.

Clients often come to our meetings with ideas, and those ideas are usually pictures of homes that have already been designed. These clients were different because they wanted something unique. The home's architecture was stunning, and my job was to add to the light that was already present. They did have a few requests: stick to a neutral, high-contrast color palette; make it modern, but keep it cozy; and figure out a way to incorporate a steel I beam, for an industrial vibe.

We started with the kitchen to influence the decisions in the rest of the great room. With the high, asymmetrical sloped ceiling, we opted for a custom stainless steel hood flanked by walnut open shelving. We wanted the ceiling to be a feature of, instead of a hindrance to, the cabinet design. To fill the open space between the top shelf and the ceiling, we installed brass task lights to illuminate the stacked plates and bowls below. The cabinets were painted black and paired with brass pulls, and we selected a pure white quartz for the waterfall-edge countertops.

Two hidden dishwashers flanked either side of the sink, which had an industrial spring faucet with a two-foot arc. We designed custom panels to conceal the Sub-Zero fridge and make it look like cabinetry. The kitchen was black, white, and brass, with hints of walnut. We hung large white, cone-shaped pendants above the fifteen-foot island, and when you sat down and looked up, you could see the brass detail on the insides of the shades.

We styled the shelves thoughtfully, with everyday glassware for easy access on the bottom and special-occasion pieces, like cake stands, on the top shelf. I found a twelve-foot vintage runner with a warm rust and navy color palette to place between the Wolf range and sink. The most striking selection was the last: we placed seven sculptural Cherner counter stools in a walnut finish across the back side of the island.

We commissioned a fifteen-foot-long, solid oak dining table to follow the length of the island and mixed cognac leather with gray wool seating in the living room. The fireplace was a six-foot-wide, double-sided opening that roared when lit. The original plans called for a stacked stone surround, but our clients felt the concept was predictable for a mountain home and a bit too inspired by a ski lodge.

Incorporating their requests had been easy until that point, but I remained stuck on how to incorporate a steel I beam. As I stared at the framing for the future fireplace, I realized the scale of the I beam would make a perfect mantel. Instead of a wall of stone, I wanted to create a paneled steel fireplace with a floating concrete hearth below. The architect wasn't happy I was changing the stone, but my job was to advocate for my clients, and they were unhappy with the original concept.

I tried to explain my idea on-site, but words couldn't communicate what was in my mind, and no one understood what I was suggesting. "Let's draw it out," I said. "I really think this will work and we'll all be happy with the result." I drove back to the office, and our team helped me flesh out the layout and dimensions.

I was able to recess a portion of the wall to carry the exterior stone inside, as the architect envisioned, but give it a natural stopping point before the fireplace began. We drew out wide steel panels surrounding the firebox, with small rivets to secure them. The steel I beam would be the mantel for hanging stockings at Christmas, and we designed a floating concrete hearth that extended the entire length of the wall to join all the materials together. The final detail on our drawing was a large antler trophy placed above the mantel. I held my breath as we sent the drawings to the clients.

"This is it!" our clients said. I was both relieved and excited to see the pieces of the home begin to fall into place.

Syd

The hard finishes were being implemented, the furniture was specified, and my team was ordering everything to ensure it would arrive on time for the big install. The contractors kept pushing the finish date, and Christmas was a few weeks away. The only item we were missing was the antler trophy for above the mantel.

I found a small-town taxidermist and went to his shop. He directed me to a pile of antlers in the back of his truck. "Pick a pretty one," he said. I selected the largest and most symmetrical pair I could find, and he delivered them to our project a few days later.

The fireplace wall that our team conceptualized became the most iconic part of our modern mountain home project.

At that time, Shea was thirty-eight weeks pregnant with our second daughter, Ivy. When the movers arrived with four truckloads of furniture, we had our design team stationed across the house with assignments like wash bedding, fold towels, add furniture pads, and stuff pillows. Shea was on her feet all day, swollen and uncomfortable.

After two years, it was time to finally see this monumental project come together. We invested in hiring a professional photographer, and he captured every angle with precision and light. Too excited to wait for the lead time of print publishing, we posted the photos to our blog and Instagram as soon as they hit our inbox.

A few months later, we received an email through the general inquiry form on our website from an editor at *Architectural Digest* who wanted to feature the project and interview Shea. Without hesitation, Shea cleared the calendar and made herself available.

When the story went live, Shea called me, her voice shaking. "Did you see it? We made the home page!"

Shea

And to think that I had originally turned down the project because I didn't feel qualified. Now it was being featured by a design publication I had admired for years. I was beginning to realize my own natural light.

nine

YOU DO YOU

When designing your own home,
stay true to your authentic self.

Syd

Shea's morning sickness with Ivy left her sitting on the studio floor most days, her chin resting on her knees. Curled in a ball, she'd take deep breaths to calm the nausea while working from her phone. She perked up when an email came through that brightened her day. It was from a producer with a television production company. He said, "I'm really good friends with one of the heads at HGTV, and they are very interested in what you guys are doing." When she read the email to me, I said, "I can't believe they even know who we are. Yeah, we should definitely talk to them."

Shea

We were naive and wooed by the production company when they name-dropped HGTV. They knew exactly what to say to hook us:

"The show will take viewers behind the scenes of your business, with a focus on design. We've gotten away from design television these days. It's a lot about construction now, but we love you guys because you are business partners and design oriented. You could share tips and tricks with viewers the same way you do on Instagram."

Syd and I were flattered that someone thought we could do our own television show. We were like, "What do we need to do to make this happen?"

Syd

It wasn't a hard sell to get us on board. Shea and I worked non-stop to establish Studio McGee, and a television show could take us beyond the world of Instagram to reach a wider audience and help our business achieve new heights. Having our own show seemed like a great way to accomplish both much faster than we ever thought possible.

I asked what the next steps might be. The producer said, "So we have to make a sizzle reel."

Shea and I looked at each another. "What's a sizzle reel?" I asked.

"We come out for a day, follow you guys around, and showcase some of your work. We'll condense that down into a one-minute video and pitch it," they said. In the conversation that followed, we discovered it wasn't quite as simple as that. They needed to shoot us doing an install in a client's house. The timing wasn't right for them to be able to capture the actual end of a project, so instead we lined up a fake install in one of our previous clients' homes.

Shea

The production company sent a small film crew from LA in a minivan full of camera equipment. They wired us with microphones and gave us a pep talk about being authentic and true to ourselves. "Syd, you're a business guy," I heard the producer say. "Plenty of couples have the designer and contractor relationship, but we just want you to be you."

They interviewed us about our origin story and had me point to design boards while bouncing Wren on my hip. "Showing your family makes you seem real," they said. They filmed us placing furniture and had Syd hang a few things on the walls. For the most part, our day stayed close to what they had prepped us for, but we were too green to realize they were setting the scene for Syd to play a handyman role.

The sizzle reel sucked us in. Even though neither of us had considered doing a television show, once we finished the sizzle reel, we both wanted it. I checked my email constantly, hoping we'd hear back from the production company. When they called and told us we'd made it through the first set of hoops, we were thrilled. We made it to the first cut round, where they film the first half of a pilot episode. If the first cut went well, they'd come back and shoot the second half of the episode, the reveal of the kitchen, to complete the pilot. After the pilot episode aired, there were still a few more hoops to jump through before landing a series, but at least we were in the process. The idea of having a Studio McGee show felt like a real possibility.

We couldn't stage a fake project for the first cut like we had for the sizzle reel. Now we had to take the cameras to an actual remodel project—a kitchen remodel, the most watched of all home renovation projects. Everyone loves a good kitchen remodel.

A few weeks before the scheduled start of filming, we posted an ad on our website asking people to submit an application to be on a potential television show with us. We sorted through hundreds of applications until we found one family that had the winning combination of personality, budget, and timing. Once the client was lined up, we established a schedule with the film crew. The plan was for them to shoot the demo, and if that went well, they'd come back to film the big reveal. We were committed to doing the entire kitchen remodel, but the production company was only interested in the first half. They just needed to get enough of a *real* project on film to pitch to the network.

We had a few conversations with the producer before their arrival for the one-day shoot. The sizzle reel was one minute, and now they needed twenty. "Don't be nervous," they told us over and over. "On the day of shooting, we just want you to be yourselves. Just do what you normally do on the job. That's what we're here to capture."

Syd

The morning of the first cut, the producer called and asked me to bring a sledgehammer to the shoot. I can't recall ever needing a sledgehammer when running the business side of Studio McGee, but apparently I needed one for the film crew. When I walked into the project house, a crew member handed me a hard hat and goggles.

"What are these for?" I asked.

"We want you to help do the demo," they said.

"You know I'm not a contractor," I said.

"That's okay," they said.

For the rest of that day of shooting, they had me play the role of the Studio McGee in-house contractor. They had me knock on walls and repeat the line "I think this is load bearing" about ten times. A camera guy dropped down to floor level to shoot me lifting the sink up out of the counter. Another camera guy filmed me throwing big chunks of debris into the dumpster and saying things like, "That was a slam dunk," and "From downtown!" I don't even play basketball.

At one point they had me stand in the middle of the kitchen and comment on how I smelled gas. There was no gas.

All the while they kept telling me, "Don't be nervous. Just be yourself. We want to capture the real you." It was like when you say to your wife, "Just calm down." It has the exact opposite effect.

Shea

My role in the first cut was to paint the picture of what the kitchen would become by pointing and saying things like, "My plan is to transform this dated seventies kitchen into a place the whole family can enjoy. This angled island has got to go. Syd, can you give me a hand?" I'd follow the same formula over and over again for each element of the kitchen. "This wall really blocks the flow of traffic into the space. Syd, is this a load-bearing wall?"

Then they'd have us stand outside together, with Syd's arm around my shoulders, talking about the construction. "I thought this was going to be a design show?" I asked. The response was that viewers were more interested in the action.

When the day of shooting finally ended, Syd and I went home and flopped on the couch, exhausted. "What just happened?" I asked.

The two of us wanted this for our business so bad that we'd lost ourselves in the process. We were told to be ourselves, but we'd spent the day being anything but. "Maybe we can persuade them to let us be ourselves if we land an actual show," Syd said. I was irritated we were in a situation where we needed permission to be authentic.

As it turns out, we didn't need to worry about changing anything. The production company contacted us and told us that HGTV—with whom we still hadn't had any direct contact—had decided to pass on our show. "We just don't understand Syd's role," was the primary feedback.

We were both like, "Are you kidding me?" It's not like Syd's role was a big mystery. We were always up front about who we were, what we did, and what our roles were. I believe this was their way of saying they didn't know how to squeeze Syd's role into their template. Syd standing there with a sledgehammer, wearing a hard hat while knocking on load-bearing walls, didn't come across as natural because that's not who he is.

We'd gotten away from our authentic selves because we were trying to become who others wanted us to be. When it fell apart, we looked at each another and vowed: never again. Television wasn't the path for us, and we committed to not lose sight of who we were as a brand and as individuals. We'd find a way to share another side of Studio McGee.

The missed TV deal was one of the best things to ever happen to us. What appeared to be another setback actually strengthened our conviction in each other, ourselves, and our business.

Syd

Having the door slammed in our faces felt like getting rejected at Market all over again. "You aren't good enough" is what I heard them say. I went through the same stages of grief we'd experienced before. Yet again, the rejection lit a fire inside of me. What infuriated me most was the fact that we didn't pursue TV—they came to us. Then they didn't want us to be us. And now we were mourning the loss of something we didn't even want in the first place. We weren't going to make that mistake again.

Shea and I knew what we were doing was significant, even if we didn't fit the formula. We moped around for a few days but realized that one of the greatest advantages of entrepreneurship was that we didn't need permission. We didn't need their permission to launch our own show, and the internet had already proven to be a powerful platform for the growth of our business. Instagram allowed us to communicate directly to our following. Why not use YouTube to do the same thing, but with a different format? For some time I'd been telling Shea that we should invest in doing video. This seemed like a perfect time to start.

Shea and I share the same reaction to rejection, and as soon as I told her about my idea to produce our own webisodes, she was all for it. We hired a contract videographer to shoot an upcoming install at a local project. Rather than try to re-create the same format of shows on home-improvement networks, we opted for short-form content, under fifteen minutes long, that focused on the design aspects of our work. The videos would be filled with tidbits of information that viewers could take and apply in their own homes.

Shea

Before we started posting regularly, we assumed our Instagram followers would tune in to our YouTube channel, and any new people we reached through YouTube would come over and follow us on Instagram. This made perfect sense to us, but we were wrong.

With Instagram, we'd built our brand through the platform and had spent years understanding what worked and what didn't. Each platform has its own unique audience, which means what works on one doesn't necessarily work on the other. If we were going to grow our brand via YouTube, we had to figure out how to best reach that audience.

Our first video was at our modern mountain home project, and it consisted entirely of beauty shots set to music. We were working with a videographer friend who made gorgeous wedding and family films, but we were all figuring out the best way to showcase design work. After we had a few portfolio videos under our belts, we decided to try talking to the camera and incorporating more progress leading up to the final reveal.

We had a small local install on the horizon and decided this was a good test run to graduate from videos to webisodes. The number one priority was actually installing all the final elements. We didn't want to add time to the process, so we moved in furniture, styled bookshelves, and ignored the camera. Then we filmed the interview separately, against a blurred backdrop of our office, and pieced the video together with a mix of install footage, interviews, and voice-over.

We used the microphone on the camera, and our voices echoed. YouTubers got straight to the point. They let us know they were unhappy with the sound quality, so we purchased individual mics. We assumed that since home-improvement shows are thirty minutes to an hour long, our condensed version should be half as long. It only took a few videos to discover that online viewers have no attention span. Viewership dropped to nothing after about ten minutes. The prospect of a big reveal at the end didn't keep people engaged. That's when we realized that if we were ever going to build a subscriber base, we needed to break up projects into a series of shorter videos. Instead of featuring an entire home at once, we would divide the webisodes by room and share them weekly, to keep people coming back for more. We still had big plans to expand our e-commerce at some point, and webisodes were a vital part of the strategy.

Syd

We knew video had huge potential, but we also weren't sure if we had enough content for a full-time videographer. As a start-up, we were conservative in our spending and developed a habit of stretching our resources as far as we could before adding people to our team. At that time, few designers were leveraging video for marketing. Although we learned with every video we produced, we also had no idea what we were doing. Hiring a full-time videographer was an opportunity to bring in an expert to further establish ourselves as a leader in the design industry and connect with our fans on a different level. We hoped this would be the case, but at that point it was too early to tell.

What we did know was that hiring people with talents Shea and I didn't possess always proved valuable in the long run. This was the same reason we hired designers with extensive AutoCAD experience and an accounting team that did more than check our bank statements. We took the leap in expanding our marketing team to include video, which has become integral to how we connect with our community.

There was a learning curve behind and in front of the camera for all of us. I had to learn to loosen up, and Shea still hasn't broken the habit of talking with her hands. In the webisodes, Shea shares insight into the how and why behind our team's designs. We distill the decisions we make for clients in their multimillion-dollar homes and show how they can be applied to any home. I'm just there for the jokes (and good looks).

Shea

About a year in, we hit our stride and became hooked on directing our own videos—and our audience was hooked too. Videos added another dimension to our work and team. Future clients could see our personalities and experience the homes we designed in their truest form, beyond photographs.

Showcasing our projects was a start, but we saw even more potential for video. We wanted to do Q&A sessions with our community, share how-to videos, and someday feature products we were selling. There was movement and music and connection.

Videos embodied our vision of teaching our fans how to make life beautiful through thoughtful design. We didn't outline steps to copy our projects verbatim: we were teaching viewers how to take principles of good design and apply them in their own way.

Our goal was to help people see that they could follow our rules about things like balance, proportion, and scale, while ultimately arriving at a unique result. A result that is deeply personal and a true reflection of one's individuality.

ten

GET TO THE NEXT LEVEL

*Let your designs evolve and
take shape over time.*

Syd

We relocated to Utah in July 2014, and in September we moved into our Pierpont office. Three months later we had our first Studio McGee holiday party, at a restaurant called Alamexo in downtown Salt Lake City. I wore a tie and told everyone to order whatever they wanted on the menu because it was our treat. Six people were there: Shea and me, our two employees, and their dates. From where we sat, we could see café lights shining through the snow flurries and our server making guacamole tableside.

The conversation was light, as we were all still getting to know one another. "Do you ski?" "Are you traveling anywhere for Christmas?"

The bonus that year was an iPhone. They thought we were the coolest bosses ever.

The next Christmas we were up to a dozen employees. Though

we couldn't afford to buy everyone iPhones, we did give them gift cards to their favorite shops.

Our team consisted of thirty employees the following year. We had outgrown the restaurant scene and decided to hire a well-known local chef to come to our new office and cook a seven-course meal. Shea set up one long banquet table with a gray tablecloth and gold chairs, and her mom crafted the floral arrangements.

The following Christmas we had sixty employees. And the next year we had somewhere around eighty.

We doubled our team size nearly every year, and we could barely hire people fast enough to keep up with the growth. The early days were exciting, and our upward trajectory made us feel there were no limits to what Shea and I could do together. We could see the day when we would open design offices in New York and Los Angeles to further establish our name in major cities. Our e-commerce business would continue to thrive, and we might even add physical stores across the country.

We never composed a formal business plan, but in a way, the lack of rigidity allowed us to pivot as conditions in the market and our lives changed. The business continued to grow organically, both in size and scope, as we listened to our instincts as well as our customers' demands. Shea and I have never considered a ceiling to our growth.

Shea

We were designing both small and big projects—living room and kitchen remodels, and entire homes from foundation to finish. We managed projects twenty miles away and two thousand miles away. Our Instagram following brought attention to our firm from all over the United States. We designed remote projects, communicating entirely through phone calls and emails. When the clients wanted me to fly out, I flew out. If someone called and asked us to design their home, we said yes. Neither Syd nor I ever took the work for granted. When you own your own business, you can't afford to coast, even for a little while.

With the ever-increasing number of projects, we hired more and more designers, all of them young and fresh out of design school. The youth of our company attracted youth, which was both an advantage and a challenge. Our team had promising talent at entry-level rates, and we were able to cultivate their artistry in the Studio McGee way, without them having any preconceived notions about what a design firm should or shouldn't be.

But having inexperienced staff also meant we had to instruct them in basic professional skills not taught in their space-planning classes. Syd and I taught crash courses in communication and time management. We had to explain that it was more efficient to set aside time to read emails instead of answering them in real time. "Otherwise you'll never be able to accomplish the task you originally set out to do," I told them. I also remember saying, "I know we don't like their existing sofa, but there is a way to be kind while also suggesting that we have a better solution." While we worked to develop their experience quickly, Syd and I micromanaged every facet of the business for the first two years.

None of our designers met with clients or designed spaces alone. They primarily focused their time on drawing, getting pricing, and pulling options for us to review together. Lead designers attended meetings with me so they could learn the trade. Syd and I knew that at some point it would be impossible for me to physically attend every call, meeting, and site visit. Our team would be ready eventually, but it was a grueling path to development.

Each initial client meeting had the same purpose: get familiar with the clients' personal style, create a design wish list, and understand how they wanted their home to function. I'd ask a lot of questions: "How many kids do you have?" "Is durability or style more important to you?" "I noticed you like blue—are there any colors you don't like?" I would leave with my head spinning and a clear vision of where to take the design.

I'd sit in a padded, white rolling chair and slide from one designer to the next, working through every inch of the drawings and shopping for every item together, until the designs felt just right. These marathon design sessions were technically for our clients but also were essential training sessions, as I taught these young designers everything I knew.

Sitting with each designer and personally overseeing every drawing took hours and even weeks, but after selling everything to start our business, our name was all we had. I felt, and still feel, personally attached to every design our team produces. These designs weren't just about our reputation—I wanted our clients to be happy. I wanted them to be smiling while washing dishes in their beautiful new kitchen sink.

Some designers churn out work because they need to pay the bills. They recycle designs and have a "quantity over quality" approach. Our problem was that we were taking a quantity *and* quality approach, and it was exhausting. Our entire business was founded on showing our work through social media. If the end result of a project doesn't represent our brand, we don't share the photographs, and that's a lost opportunity for us to expand our business.

All of this placed immense pressure on me, and our young team, to continuously put out beautiful work at an unprecedented pace. It was becoming increasingly difficult to maintain high standards when we had forty or more projects going on at once. Everyone was overwhelmed.

In our first year alone, I attended every meeting, had calls with contractors, made shopping trips, did site visits, stayed in contact with clients, styled every surface at installs, took photos, posted to Instagram, and wrote our blog. I'd go to the studio every morning, leave at two in the afternoon, trade off parent duties with Syd, spend quality time with Wren, eat dinner, and put Wren to bed. Then Syd and I would work past midnight, on our laptops in bed, to prepare for the next day. We'd tweak our service offerings and contracts and discuss how we were going to make improvements while simultaneously keeping up with everything that was happening or coming down the pipeline. Because we were both exhausted, our late-night work sessions often became strained and led to arguments.

We constantly asked ourselves how we could be better and do better. We had no consultants or managers or C-level executives to bounce ideas off of. *We* were the company's leadership team. At times there may have been tension, but our unwillingness to settle for status quo was formative in shaping our business as we know it today.

Syd

Yes, we hired people to do what we couldn't do well ourselves, but we also couldn't afford to hire everyone we needed from the start. We focused on growing the design team and later added operational team members, adding staff as we could afford it. In the meantime, I billed clients, set up accounts with vendors, managed textile production, and also was the head of accounting, HR, payroll, and screening all potential clients.

I came from an industry where software made everything more efficient, so our organization wasn't as personnel heavy. Reviewing applications and interviewing, hiring, and onboarding new employees took up most of my day, and what little time was left I spent in the weeds, keeping up with administrative needs. With so much happening, I lost sight of the business from a high-level perspective.

Shea

In the beginning we had a certain pride that came with working long hours and doing anything and everything to make the business succeed. Rather than take a paycheck, we continually poured every penny back in, knowing that in the long run the investment would be worth it.

Well, Syd said it would be worth it.

About a year after launching Studio McGee, I became impatient. We worked longer hours than anyone in the office while also being the lowest-paid team members. I'd spend all day designing dream homes in soothing color palettes for other people, then come home to a bright purple front door. We did our best not to be resentful when our staff took paid days off or went on vacation. But when we received an employment verification call from a mortgage company for one of our designers who was buying a house, it was hard not to wonder what we were doing all of this for. We were providing proof for an employee to purchase a home when we'd been denied one for ourselves.

Syd kept telling me we'd eventually get there, but I was running out of gas. Then I found out I was pregnant with Ivy. I was elated, but also very tired. I announced the pregnancy on Mother's Day at our annual family barbecue, where the guys are in charge of making dinner for the girls. Since I had just taken the test earlier that morning, I'd planned to wait a few weeks before sharing the news. However, when we were gathered around my parents' kitchen, eating cheeseburgers, I let it slip. I was too excited to keep it a secret and a bit nervous about how we were going to juggle everything with two kids. We were barely keeping up as it was.

I was so nauseated that the feeling would wake me in the middle of the night, but I kept pushing through. Some days I'd come home from the studio to nap on the couch while Wren sat on my feet and watched *Daniel Tiger's Neighborhood*. Other days I'd wait for Wren to nap so I could watch *Gossip Girl*.

After the move from our kitchen table to our first studio, Syd and I would take turns being at home with Wren. The only overlap in our work schedule was late at night, and our discussions about problems to fix, improvements to be made, and paychecks for ourselves often led us in circles. There is value in pressing pause to make progress, but we hadn't learned that yet.

During this time, my brother had finished his master's degree program at the University of British Columbia and was interviewing for a job close to us. His wife, Laura, and their baby girl, Piper, visited us while he was at his final interview, before they extended a formal offer. Piper and Wren were a year apart, and we put them in their strollers and walked around the neighborhood.

Laura has always been the sister I never had. She could tell I was putting on a brave face and offered to help. "We're moving here soon," she said. "I'd love to watch Wren while you're at the studio. She and Pipes will be besties." Her offer thrilled and relieved me. It was a direct answer to my prayers for help. Torn between my desire to be a loving mother and to chase our entrepreneurial dreams, I was running myself into the ground, which wasn't doing our family, our business, or me any good.

To this day, Laura is the single most important team member of Studio McGee. We always say we would relocate our entire business to keep her in our lives. Her Little Mermaid impressions are tops, and I don't worry when I'm away because she loves our kids as her own.

The help at home changed our work schedule, but Syd and I managed to fill in the extra time with more stress. I became critical of his handling of the business, and he questioned my ability to train our designers. We could feel our relationship drifting toward rugged terrain, and we needed a break. We hadn't taken a day off since our babymoon, when I was pregnant with Wren. Since we still lived off our savings, we didn't have extra money for a trip.

"Should we drive to California and stay at your parents'?" I asked. "We'd have to pay for gas, but the stay would be free." Syd said we had racked up enough points through our credit cards to cover two plane tickets and five days at an all-inclusive Cancún resort. We only had to get two tickets because Wren was still small enough to sit on our laps.

I couldn't wait to get away. We needed time to be a family without work pressures. With the endless projects, new employees, and constant burden to do more, while watching our savings account dwindle each month, work had become all-consuming. Syd and I had no boundaries. We talked about business every single waking moment. Every conversation was some variation of, "What could we do better? Why did this client respond like this? Are they upset?"

We needed this break. However, our business was fragile, and we knew we couldn't completely cut ourselves off. Syd and I both packed our laptops, just in case we needed to take care of something. Syd's cell phone also doubled as the company phone. All new business inquiries and shipping notifications went straight to him. Neither of us thought about transferring his calls while we were gone. We also convinced ourselves there wouldn't be many work calls, since our team knew we were going on our first vacation since launching the company. They'd give us some space.

Syd

The phone rang right after we landed in Cancún. I told Shea, "I need to take this really quick." We were walking around the airport, trying to find our hotel shuttle, with me on the phone and Shea trying to push a stroller, carry a car seat, and juggle our suitcases. She kept giving me a look that told me to hang up the phone and help her, but I couldn't wrap up the call. I can't remember if it was a vendor trying to arrange delivery at a project or one of our employees calling about billing. Whatever it was, it seemed important at the time because the business depended on it.

All the while, Shea got increasingly frustrated with me. "It'll be just another minute and we can get started on our vacation," I said.

The next call came shortly thereafter. Then another. And another. It wasn't just my phone that kept blowing up. Shea's rang constantly as well.

We did our best to settle into vacation mode. After we arrived at the hotel, we unloaded the suitcases in our room, grabbed the camera, and headed to the pool. "No calls while at the pool, okay?" Shea told me. "Absolutely," I said. We didn't even take our phones with us.

Yet work didn't disappear when the phones were stashed. "I need to post something on Instagram," Shea said. That turned into me doing a photo shoot of Shea, trying to get an angle she approved of while seven months pregnant. "You can't just snap one and then call it good," she said. "Can't you see my double chin in that angle?"

When we returned to the room, we both had missed calls. Wren was worn out from the pool, so we put her down for a nap and opened our laptops. Both of our inboxes were overflowing. "Okay, let's just respond to these and then we'll go to dinner," I said. More emails were waiting after dinner. And our conversations stayed stuck on the same kind of work discussions we had every night.

Each day we were determined to do better, to be on vacation rather than working long-distance. Then the calls came in. They were basic questions like, "Do you like the height of this chandelier?" and logistics matters like, "Sir, I need to schedule a delivery tomorrow morning."

I wanted to yell, "Leave us alone and figure it out!" But we hadn't set clear boundaries or trained our team to solve problems on their own. When our team came to us with a question, we often fixed the problem and moved on, without taking advantage of the teachable moment.

At one point I became so frustrated I said to Shea, "Would you just put your phone away and enjoy this vacation?"

"I can't because I have to take care of this if we're still going to be in business when we get back," Shea shot back. The conversation went downhill from there. What I heard, even though Shea didn't say it, was that if I hadn't quit my job, we wouldn't have been in this mess in the first place.

I chose to disregard the fact that our problem was a good one to have: we were struggling to keep up with a business that a year prior we didn't even know would succeed. I still carried a natural, implied guilt that I had put us in such a tenuous position. I hated to see Shea with her head barely above water. I wanted to fix our situation, but I needed to listen first.

Shea

Work was our life, and we'd forgotten how to do anything outside of it. I couldn't relax, even though we needed to. When we spent a day in Tulum, we walked around town, stopping at every fruit stand and wandering through boutiques. It was on my bucket list to visit the famous Coqui Coqui hotel and see their pared-down, white plaster walls contrasting against dark-stained beams and hammocks dripping with fringe. I hoped to bring home a bottle of their eponymous perfume that smells like the Yucatán, with top notes of coconut and bitter greens.

We found the hotel, and instead of soaking it in, I had to find something to post on Instagram, to show how this trip was inspiring my creativity—even though the opposite was happening. On our walk through this exotic town, I spent most of my time on the phone with one of our designers. By the time I hung up, I had to find something to shoot because I'd committed to posting every day. No excuses.

When our last day at the resort rolled around, we realized we'd blown our entire trip. I looked over at Syd in the infinity pool while Wren splashed around in her floaties, happy as could be.

"We can't keep this up," I told him. "I feel more stressed now than I did the day we left. We don't even remember how to have fun together anymore."

"I know," Syd said. "This isn't working. I'd rather step away from the business to make our marriage stronger than live like this."

"You're kidding me, right?" I snapped. "You can't quit on me."

For the first time since our move, we had a gut-level conversation about what we needed from each other to see each other as more than business partners. The excitement of being entrepreneurs with a skyrocketing business had faded. This was our life now, and we needed to make it sustainable before one or both of us burned out.

"I care too much about design. That part of our business isn't scalable, and we can't keep saying yes to everything that comes along. I've hit a wall, and I just can't do that. Besides, I want to enjoy being a wife and a mother. I'm not willing to sacrifice that for a business," I said.

I wish I could say everything changed as soon as we got home. Of course, it didn't.

I was on a hospital bed, waiting to be wheeled into the operating room to deliver Ivy, when my phone dinged. I picked it up to see an email from a designer about sofa options for a client in California.

But instead of silencing my phone, I turned it off.

The Cancún trip was a turning point for us. We'd have to grind through some tough months ahead, but we were determined to take our business to the next level. And for us, that meant taking a step back to move forward.

Holding Ivy for the first time refocused my priorities. I wanted to be present for my family, to uplift and empower them. This was the same approach we needed to take with our business.

Syd

Changing our approach to how we managed our business wasn't the only epiphany we had because of our failed vacation. We also planned to pivot our attention to building a retail division, which we'd tried to start in the beginning. But this time we wouldn't take no for an answer.

eleven

TAKE RISKS

*A good designer knows when to play
it safe and when to take risks.*

Shea

Even in our days spent dreaming from a spare bedroom office, Syd had the foresight to know we needed to expand beyond design services. He told me many times: "Shea, I know you love it, but the way you design is not scalable." He was right, but we also didn't have a promising alternative, so we maintained focus on our design business.

Not long after Ivy was born, we hired a consultant to review our overall business and look for opportunities to increase profitability. The consultant concluded that I was a bottleneck. "Well, I'm the bottleneck that makes our projects look really good," I shot back. The consultant then suggested we replicate designs. "Why don't you come up with premade, prepackaged designs and sell those one hundred times over?" he asked. I was offended. The purity of what we did would be lost. The consultant went on to say that if his first suggestion wouldn't work, we should hire a large team of designers so I could step back from the process and allow the business to flourish. I was again offended.

I viewed a refusal to delegate as a strength. I single-handedly managed every task alone for years—I had a clear vision of not only the end product but the way it should be executed. My resistance to letting go was largely fueled by my ego. I thought, *If my name is going to be on a project, I'm going to be involved in it.* However, the pride in my work was also the very thing hindering our ability to move forward.

And that's why from the onset, Syd knew our design services were only scalable to a certain degree. I tried to convince myself otherwise. When we first started talking about someday having offices in New York and Los Angeles, I thought I might be able to hire designers who shared my exact vision and process. However, deep down I knew that wasn't realistic or fair. As hard as it was for me to admit, if we were going to continue expanding the business, I had to learn to delegate and find a different avenue to scale.

In our earliest conversations, Syd and I talked about creating a brand. We were both enamored by companies that connected with their customers, cared about product design, and told a story. We discussed our mutual love for magazines and catalogs and wanted to create a hybrid model to promote our products. We could share interior design knowledge while simultaneously selling product. This concept supported our desire to bridge the gap between high-end design and approachability.

When we'd tried to open an e-commerce store at the same time we launched Studio McGee, we'd been turned down, with great disdain, at both the Las Vegas and High Point Markets. Vendors would've rather foregone income than let us carry their products on our site. Although the interior design industry is fashion forward, they're slow-moving with technology. They viewed the internet as the Wild West. However, Syd was especially committed to e-commerce and never gave up on the idea. But we had to wait until the right time.

Syd

Over the years I've learned that deviations from our original plans ultimately fall into place even better than we'd intended. For instance, take our experience with the throw pillows. We had our fig-leaf print and four other patterns Shea and I had created: striped, floral, geometric, and an abstract urchin. The designs were complete, the fabric was printed, and all twenty-five hundred yards were wrapped on large bolts in our garage. The longer we took to find a workroom to cut and sew the pillows, the longer it would take to recoup our investment. I went to upholstery shops all over Salt Lake City to find someone who could make these pillows, without success. The job was either too small or too large, or they weren't equipped to sew with our exposed gold zippers.

Finally I walked into a wedding dress shop down the street from our Pierpont office. "This is crazy," I said, "but do you know anyone who could sew a few hundred throw pillows?" To my surprise one of the workers said, "Yeah. I know someone who used to do custom drapes. I'll talk to her." One conversation led to another, and I'd found our person. Instead of a dedicated website for pillows, the "store" was a tab on our blog that linked to a simple shop interface. And just like that, we were in the business of selling pillows.

Shea and I recouped our original investment within three months. We added patterns seasonally and discontinued the lowest performers. I wrapped, boxed, and shipped the pillows myself. Eventually we hired help to fulfill and ship orders, and the pillow side of the business became self-sustaining.

Scaling back from developing an entire home store to only selling pillows and down inserts may have felt like a compromise, yet in the long run this step was the opposite. No, a pillow business was not *the* dream. But by doing something instead of nothing, we kept the dream alive. If we'd launched a design firm and an e-commerce brand in tandem, our attention would have been divided, and we likely would have failed at one or both businesses.

After we returned from Cancún, Shea and I agreed it was time to take another risk. I calculated that we needed to invest at least $100,000 in web development, and another $60,000 in product as initial inventory, to launch our new business. The website had to both reflect our aesthetic and be able to handle the traffic. We still hadn't changed our minds about going into debt, so we pulled money out of the business to invest in this potential revenue stream. Up to that point, taking risks had paid off. Selling our home, moving to a less expensive location, manufacturing pillows, and growing our team had all succeeded. I believed we'd experience a positive return on this investment as well.

Shea

Brands with personality and perspective inspired us. Most online furniture sites either were an extension of existing brick-and-mortar chains or felt like a warehouse jammed with thousands of products.

If you wanted a chair, you typed "chair" into a search field and waited for hundreds of options to pop up. These sites lacked an aesthetic or viewpoint. Their only goal was to present as many options as possible with as little work as possible. All the generic product photos came directly from vendors and didn't inspire shoppers to create an atmosphere in their own homes. The product selections were driven by search terms rather than practicing interior designers.

In contrast, we wanted design to drive our e-commerce brand, not the other way around. Our small business couldn't compete with the major players, but we didn't intend to. We'd develop a curated site offering products we already featured in our projects. Every Instagram post for the past two years was filled with questions like, "Where is that from?" so we already had interest from our audience.

I handpicked products that reflected our design style, not bestsellers on other sites. We'd manufacture some of the products, and others would be sourced from vendors. But either way, they all needed to feel like they belonged in a Studio McGee home. Though we couldn't scale our business to provide design services for all of our followers, we could curate a collection for them to achieve a similar look.

The more Syd and I talked about our ambitions for the online store, the more we appreciated that we hadn't been able to launch the full e-commerce site when we started Studio McGee. The traditional route to launching a brand is to come up with a name, produce products, launch a website, and build an audience. Our path was the opposite. We cultivated a following that trusted our design perspective and then launched a brand. And this built-in trust was established only because our original plan didn't go according to plan.

We wanted a seamless connection between the businesses. However, we also wanted the online store to have a distinct identity from Studio McGee and its design services. McGee was a recognizable connection, and the addition of "& Co." was just that—an expansion of the brand.

Design through any platform is my passion; McGee & Co. is Syd's passion. He stepped in and did anything and everything to make the e-commerce site successful. Once we started working on launching the store, he reminded me of what I was like when my first few clients hired me. And watching him work made me think back to the years he'd spent trying to figure out what he wanted to do with his career and the rest of his life. With the online store launch, even with all its problems, he had found his place.

Syd

No matter how appealing our online store looked, it was only as good as the platform. We'd been using a Squarespace template to sell our pillows, but I wanted something more flexible. Templates may be easy to use but can make a site appear generic.

I called several friends working for companies with large e-commerce sites, and they all recommended the same platform. One friend also recommended a web designer in Chicago who built sites for less money than agencies typically charged. We had developed a wireframe and prepared the graphic design assets when I called him to work through the details. We hoped to launch the site in the summer, to have things up and running before the holiday shopping season. A few months seemed like enough buffer to work through bugs on the site or in fulfillment.

From my conversations with the web designer, he seemed to have a solid understanding of the scope of work and our projected timeline. Our website was underway, so it was time to revisit all of the people who had turned us down two years prior.

This time around, our brand was more established and recognized in the design industry, and we had a portfolio of projects featuring the vendors' products. We had proof that we would do their products justice and had demand from our audience to sell the items we were using in clients' homes. Still, I knew it wouldn't be easy.

We returned to High Point Market, and I pitched our e-commerce venture to vendors. They already liked us because we were consistent customers, so I tried to lean into that selling point. "It's a curated site where we sell to the general public the products we already use in our projects," I said over and over. "That way, when our Instagram followers ask where they can buy the items they see in our posts, we can tell them they can purchase them directly from us." I thought it was a great pitch with a strong value proposition.

"We only sell to brick-and-mortar stores," I heard numerous times again. I understood where they were coming from. These companies had dealt with brick-and-mortar stores for decades, and they didn't want to deviate from a system that worked. The last thing they wanted was someone new coming in, undercutting prices, and dismantling long-standing relationships. I explained that wasn't our intention—we weren't a discount site. "We aren't interested in opening up to online stores," was the answer I heard more times than I could count.

Thankfully, not everyone shut us down. A few sales reps we worked with for Studio McGee believed in what we were doing. I showed them mock-ups of our site and explained how it would coordinate with our designs and our Instagram audience. Some said, "Okay, let's talk," right away. Others needed to be convinced, but they didn't slam the door immediately, so there was still hope.

"I can't make a call like this," several told me. I always responded, "I understand that, but I know there is someone who can." McGee & Co. was my bookshelf, and Market was my ladder. I'd work my way up each rung until I found someone who was willing to listen to us and had the authority to make decisions.

"We will adhere to your policies," I told them. "I want you to know that we already have customer traffic. They're waiting for us to launch, and they will buy. This will be good for your brand and it will be good for us." Everyone was initially resistant, but I kept pushing. We still heard no more often than yes. But a few doors cracked open was all we needed.

Shea

By this time we had finally moved out of our Pierpont office and into a brand-new space located in a posh neighborhood south of Salt Lake City called Holladay. A dentist had recently completed the new building and occupied the lower level. He left the top floor completely untouched: it was big and open with lots of windows and plywood floors. The building was essentially designed as a box, with twelve-foot-high windows and 360-degree views. We had a clear view of Mount Olympus, and the late-afternoon sun glared on our computer screens.

We almost passed up this office because at twenty-three

hundred square feet, it was way more room than we needed. But it was cheery and bright, and the empty shell provided me an opportunity to select everything from scratch. What minimal wall space there was between the windows, we painted white. We repurposed our brass pendants from Pierpont and added twelve more. The bathrooms were clean, and the conference room had drywall to the ceiling. We were beginning to feel legitimate.

Our dream partnership was with a lighting company I use in nearly every home we design. Many people ridiculed us for even thinking that working with them was a possibility, but one influential person at the company followed us on Instagram and noticed how quickly our business grew year after year. He arranged a phone call with the owner.

Syd and I paced the new conference room while waiting for the owner to join the call. We tried to explain our vision. "We have no intention of just throwing up every photo of the light fixtures you manufacture," I said. "We will style the lights in our own way, the same way our community is used to seeing them on Instagram." The owner wanted to know how we could do that with all of their products. "We won't feature all your products, only those we use in our designs. It's a curated site," I explained.

After a long conversation, we finally heard the words we hoped for: "I think y'all are onto something. Yes, you can carry our products."

However, it wasn't a blanket yes to use everything we wanted to sell. It was more like permission to start small and see what happened. That didn't matter to us. A yes was a yes. A few other furniture vendors changed their tune when they heard we had a yes from this lighting company.

I filled out the rest of the McGee & Co. online catalog with various items, like artwork, vases, and other accessories. We would do the fulfillment on all the smaller items, and the large pieces would ship directly from the manufacturer to the customer's doorstep.

Syd

After lining up enough product to launch our site, I was eager to go live. However, every time I called our web designer, he told me the site wasn't ready yet. I'd call a few days later. Same response. This continued for weeks, until I finally told him we were out of time. We had recently hired a director of e-commerce to oversee the site, and we had to launch now.

On August 18, 2016, McGee & Co. opened for business. Our ambitious goal was to do $100,000 in monthly revenue sometime before the end of the year. Before the launch, our best month of pillow sales had been $35,000. Within four months, we wanted to triple our best month of the last two years.

Sales poured in, and we reached our goal within weeks. Until the sales suddenly stopped. The server had gone off-line. I called our web developer, and he assured me he'd have it fixed in no time. Sales started pouring in again, until they stopped a second time. We ran some tests and discovered that the shopping cart function had gone down. Customers could drop items into their cart, but they couldn't check out. I called the developer again. He assured me, again, that he'd have the site working quickly. Sales started pouring in yet again, until they stopped for the third time.

Often these breakdowns happened in the middle of the night. I stayed up all hours messaging with our e-commerce director, trying to catch problems before we lost the next day's sales. We'd refresh the sales numbers every few minutes, and if we saw a gap longer than an hour, we knew something else was going wrong.

The constant breakdowns continued into September. Our developer would fix the problems, only to have the same problems keep erupting. By this point we had poured at least $90,000 into the site development, but I started to think we needed to cut our losses and find a new platform.

Our e-commerce director reached the same conclusion before I did. She came to me in late September, sat me down, and recommended we do something drastic: "We need to pull the site off-line and rebuild it."

Less than a month after we launched, we moved the entire store off-line, hired a new developer, and started over. We got the site back online by November 1, but this second rollout wasn't entirely problem-free either. The site didn't crash, but we had to tweak the image sizes. They were so large that the site took minutes instead of seconds to load. Additionally, the search button was generating unrelated results for a while, so we turned it off. In spite of all the problems, the site was up and running, and we were ready to fill orders.

Our office had a room in the basement where we planned to store and ship products. I went to Costco and bought racks to build shelving, and our part-time employee, who helped with shipping, increased her hours to include accessories under her purview. We didn't set up a SKU system because our assortment was small enough to fit on a few shelves. We'd taken a big risk and invested heavily in our website, but an underlying self-doubt caused us to play it safe with inventory and staffing. When it launched, we were grossly underprepared for the astounding response to McGee & Co.

twelve

FORM AND FUNCTION

| *Seek solutions to challenges in a*
beautiful and livable way. |

Shea

As we unpacked our inventory and placed vases, boxes, and picture frames in neat rows, I was reminded of our garage in California, where we had done the same a few years earlier. Syd had assembled a metal rack for me to store decorative objects and accessories for client projects, and I always set aside a few treasures for myself as well.

It took me a year and a few scrapes to build my decor stockpile. After my first design experience styling bookshelves, I realized that collecting pieces over time helped alleviate the rush leading up to an install. I would shop thrift stores, boutiques, and warehouse sales. A neighbor would hear from a friend who heard from a friend that a designer home brand was hosting a warehouse sale, and the news spread through our town. It would take a mountain to stand between me and steeply discounted

157

lamps, furniture, vases, and mirrors. And even then I'd figure out a way to climb it.

I'd wake up as the sun started to peer over the grassy hill behind our house, fold down the back seat of my car, and crawl through the morning traffic past Dana Point, Irvine, and Long Beach, then finally arrive at an unmarked warehouse in LA. The loading dock doors were wide open, and thousand-dollar lamps lined the pavement. Signs with handwritten numbers set the pricing structure for the morning: table lamp bases, $200; shades, $30; ottomans, $100. Prices were less than half the retail cost, and I could already see women in Lululemon leggings and Ray-Bans hovering over piles to stake their claims.

I'd start surveying the sale before I even locked the car and make a beeline to the action. Once I picked up a large recycled glass vase and a woman from ten yards away yelled, "That's my pile!" I learned to grab items first and decide later. After weaving through the maze, I'd admire my pile of mango wood boxes, oversized ceramic vases, rattan baskets, a mercury glass lamp, and a round, leather captain's mirror. I knew to bring cash and would pull an envelope out of my wallet as the cashier tallied my order on a slip of paper.

To keep my finds safe, I'd wrap the vases in T-shirts and secure lamps with a seat belt. I'd call Syd on my way home, excited to tell him about all the money I saved by shopping the sale; then I would organize my styling inventory in neat rows at the back of our garage.

Syd

As the McGee & Co. orders rolled in, our one-person fulfillment team created her own assembly line and updated the queue each morning in the basement. She'd print packing slips, tape boxes, pull items from the racks, Bubble Wrap as needed, place tissue paper with an *M* sticker on top, and stack the boxes in the lobby to wait for the next UPS pickup. Shipping pillow covers was one thing: you'd fold it into thirds and half again, place it in a branded poly bag, and it was good to go. Wrapping breakables was another. They required additional packaging and, therefore, more time per order. We also learned the hard way that certain items couldn't share a box. Concrete bookends and marble objects didn't mingle well with others, regardless of the wrapping.

She would arrive in the morning and take the elevator to the basement. At the end of the day, the elevator doors would open, and I'd say, "Hey! How's everything going down there?" For days, the response was, "We're almost caught up!" This continued until I started to suspect that we would never catch up, because orders were gaining speed. One day I went to the basement and saw rows and rows of open boxes lining the hallway, each box with a packing slip waiting to be filled out. I felt terrible that I hadn't seen she needed help, and now we were behind.

All of my attention had been focused on our broken website, but other parts of our operation were devolving while my head was turned. Our site was breaking, and so were we. After spending more than $100,000 on an unusable website, I was sick. Even if the web experience was poor, I had fooled myself into thinking that at least we were delivering beautiful products in a timely manner. And now, even that wasn't true. We didn't want to disappoint the followers we'd worked years to cultivate a relationship with. They trusted our design advice, commented on every post, and were the reason we were able to establish a name for ourselves in an industry that initially didn't welcome us.

When we took the site off-line to rebuild it, we moved out of the basement and into a third-party fulfillment center that was shipping orders for other local businesses. Their wheelhouse was T-shirts, watches, and swimsuits, but they assured us they could adapt to handle our fragile inventory. It didn't matter how beautiful our European glass mason jars were if they arrived in pieces. I reemphasized the importance of attention to detail in packaging and that their team was now an extension of our brand. "We don't have a physical store, so this is the only touchpoint with our customers," I said.

Shea

It was an enormous relief to have an actual shipping specialist take over the process so we could focus on site improvements, design, and marketing. But when we played secret shopper to ensure proper packing techniques were employed, we found out they weren't delivering on what they promised. Some vases had ten layers of Bubble Wrap and others had one. Return rates on broken items were rising, and we were losing money on the inventory. Our staff was concerned and provided constructive feedback to the fulfillment company over and over and over. Still, our inventory was dwindling from damages, orders were being overlooked, and we were losing future return customers.

So we moved to another fulfillment center. The tape machines were shiny and the racks stacked forty feet in the air were meticulously labeled. We were working with the best operation in the valley and trusted our items were in good hands.

They were in good hands, all right. When our team started

noticing that the physical inventory didn't match our systems, they went to the warehouse offices to address the issues. They were shocked to find the lobby handsomely decorated with McGee & Co. decor—the decor missing from our inventory. If this was going on, what else was missing? Our team combed through invoices to find they were filled with inaccuracies, inflated shipping rates, and additional storage charges for pallets of product we couldn't find. Soon, we were banned from coming to the warehouse where our products were stored. And all of the invitations to courtside seats at the Utah Jazz games began to make more sense.

The breach of trust devastated all of us. Our business wasn't just about Syd and me anymore—we had a team to take care of, and we needed each other to succeed. Their determination to persevere touched me, and I could see this was a formative moment in building a culture of resolve. Syd and I could either yell and scream at those who had wronged us (believe me, we wanted to), or we could focus inward, rally our team, and take action. But Syd and I didn't need to rally our employees: our McGee & Co. team was growing each week, and this shakedown bonded us together with a unified goal to make McGee & Co. into a company we could all be proud of.

Syd

After the Christmas rush, our team sacrificed their winter break to help organize twenty-four thirty-foot semis full of products to relocate to what would soon be our own warehouse. When we realized the extent of the duplicity of our previous fulfillment center, we knew it was time to ship products ourselves.

Thanks to every misstep along the way, we had collected a long list of what not to do. We had far outgrown the basement, and if we were lucky, our items would have SKUs this time. After looking at real estate listings for a few months, we had found a new warehouse complex about fifteen minutes from our office and knocked down a wall to join two spaces together. Half would be dedicated to inventory, and the other side would allow room for growth.

We also planned to create a large photo shoot area for product photography. We built a twenty-foot wall on casters, with decorative molding and light oak floors, to serve as a backdrop for shooting vignettes and visual website assets. The movable wall could be oriented so the light hit the products with just the right amount of luminosity. Our visual merchandising team could walk through the opening in the wall to pull products as they were being unloaded from the dock and shoot photos of them, so we could launch product on McGee & Co. quicker and more efficiently than ever before.

We'd never again need to ask permission to be in the same room as our own products. And more important, if we noticed inefficiencies or shortcomings, we had the power to make improvements.

We taught ourselves about racking systems and forklifts, and researched the benefits of packing peanuts versus Bubble Wrap. We hired staff, displayed OSHA posters, and recounted thousands of items. Our marketing team printed newsletters and packaging inserts that the third-party fulfillment centers had frowned upon. We had more control over the utility and beauty of our packaging, and items broke a hell of a lot less.

The initial setback led to solutions, which led to improvements for both our team and the customer. At one point a team member said to me, "That was painful, but I love knowing our products are in the right hands." We would have missed the opportunity for growth as a team if we had skipped the struggle.

Shea

As we built beyond a few rows deep into our inventory and my wandering eye moved on to new styles, it occurred to us that we could be hosting our own warehouse sales. The very type of sales I'd swarmed as a new designer, when I'd leave with an adrenaline rush and as a bigger fan of the brand. I loved design but wouldn't have been able to afford those designer items any other way, and I wanted to give others the same opportunity. Also, it would allow us to move stale inventory and recoup the money to invest in future endeavors.

Our team devised a strategy to host twice-yearly warehouse sales, and we do our best to make it an event. There are food trucks and music, and our team parties through the madness. We post an announcement on Instagram with the time, place, and instructions to BYOT—bring your own truck. The first sale was during a blizzard, but people still came. The second sale was on the hottest day of the year, but still, people came. By the third sale we had hit our stride, with larger signage and more team members tallying to check out people faster.

Before we cut the ribbon and let people loose, sneaker-clad shoppers, wagons in tow, form a line around the corner. For weeks leading up to the event, our team fills tables with blankets, baskets, trays, garlands, and bowls. They line up rows of armoires and barstools, with price tag stickers for easy shopping. All wearing

Team McGee shirts, our designers are stationed throughout the hangar-sized warehouse, prepared to answer questions about rug sizes and pillow combinations, while our operational teams are ready to check out customers. Our marketing director will count down over the bullhorn, and the four-hour frenzy begins. Dust from vintage rugs as well as feathers puff into the air as people sprint from one corner to the next yelling, "That's my pile!"

We have continued this tradition since our first full year of McGee & Co. I'm overjoyed to witness the madness through the loading dock doors of our own warehouse. But during our third warehouse event, as I stood in the middle of wives hollering at their husbands to pull up the truck, it occurred to me that these sales were the only face-to-face interaction we had with our community. They had cheered us on since the announcement of Studio McGee from our living room in California, but the relationship was all function and no form.

Syd

Shea and I returned to Orange County as often as possible. We'd pack our suitcases, the girls' suitcases, a stroller, two car seats, a portable Pack 'n Play, and a tote bag filled with a day's worth of snacks for the eighty-minute flight to John Wayne Airport for a three-day getaway. We'd visit my parents, play at the beach, and stop at Sidecar Doughnuts for a half-dozen box of their infamous butter-and-salt doughnuts.

No trip to Sidecar Doughnuts was complete without walking across the street to my favorite surf shop, full of classic, almond-shaped surfboards that looked as good on the wall as they did cutting through the water. A classic beach cruiser was propped in the window, and they played Led Zeppelin and Lou Reed from a speaker at the front desk.

During one of our excursions, I perused the T-shirts while the girls ate their doughnuts. Shea said she'd be back in a minute, and out of the corner of my eye I saw her walk across the parking lot and disappear into a wall of green. When she came back she said, "Did you know about the cute shop next door? I don't know how I ever missed it."

Shea

I'd noticed a vine-covered building with a glossy black Dutch door propped open, two potted kumquat trees flanking the entrance, and a hand-painted sign above the door that read Heritage Mercantile. I walked into the tiny shop, which smelled like sandalwood and citrus. It was warm, but I could feel the fan circulating the breeze drifting in through the open windows. The floors were hand-painted with a gray-and-white octagon pattern reminiscent of French tiles, and in the center of the shop an antique farmhouse table displayed delicate jewelry and stacked coffee table books.

I chose a thin, hammered gold ring from the table and walked by the apothecary section with lotions, soaps, and piles of stone-washed linen aprons before arriving at the counter. "Your shop is adorable," I said to the woman at the register. "Do you mind if I take a picture of your front entrance and tag you on Instagram? More people need to know about your store."

We started following each other on Instagram, and two years

later, about a month after one of our warehouse sales, I received a message: "Hi, Shea! I'm going to be moving out of Heritage to focus on other things, but this space is so special I want someone to move in who will do it justice."

Was this really happening?

I called Syd immediately. "This is our chance!" I told him. "We've always been nervous to commit to a store location, but this is the perfect chance to test it out. You know you can't say no to this."

This was our opportunity to give customers a way to be immersed in our brand. To touch our products and feel, on a small scale, what it was like to step into a home we'd designed. Plus, there were doughnuts across the street. If it were any other locale, I knew Syd would shoot down the proposition. He was vocal about his opposition to brick-and-mortar retail, with the long lease commitment and high overhead. He was right, but he also knew I'd long wanted to open a shop.

For me, opening a physical store wasn't about money—it was about creating a sensory experience for our customers. Walking into a small shop or boutique on vacation, or when I needed a moment of escape, always brought me joy. If flipping through cookbooks, smelling candles, and running my hand over linen pillows was a bright spot for me, surely our fans would feel the same way.

At only five hundred square feet, the shop was one open room with a small closet in the corner and a crow's nest loft above, where the previous shop owner's daughter did her homework. The space was too small to be a furniture showroom, but I envisioned customers coming in to grab a gift for their friend and a little pick-me-up for themselves.

Although we lived in a different state, our familiarity with the area made managing a shop from afar seem more feasible. Plus, the contract was flexible, so I had hope.

I prepared a list of convincing arguments, but I didn't even need to use them. Syd just said, "All right—tell me what it's going to cost to build out the space."

Syd

I tried to play it cool, but I was stoked to have my own piece of California again. And even if the shop could only fit a table and a few chairs, it also provided a great work-around with vendors who wanted to know if we had a brick-and-mortar store.

We flew out to take measurements and meet with the contractor while our girls twirled around the empty space and climbed the ladder to the loft. "I don't think I realized the walls are painted cinder block," Shea said. "How are we going to hang things?" This was going to require more than a simple makeover.

Because of the shop's small footprint, I'd assumed we wouldn't be doing much remodeling. We didn't need to knock down any walls, but Shea said we needed to build upward to maximize the space. Shea's designs called for vertical white shiplap to cover the cinder block and to draw the eye toward the vaulted ceilings. Although she loved the painted floors, she opted for wide oak planks to act as a neutral palette to highlight our rugs. She even designed a nonfunctioning kitchenette, complete with a bridge faucet and marble countertops with open shelves for display. "The more product we can feature, the better," she said. "We want people to walk in and feel like they're coming home."

The wall between the front bay windows provided the perfect

setting for a built-in to showcase and rotate products. We built a new cash wrap with drawers for storage, and held our breath as our contractor drilled each individual McGee & Co. letter onto the back wall. We toted the kids back and forth between Salt Lake City and Costa Mesa to check on the progress, and after four months, the Dutch door was open and we were in business.

Shea

On opening night we hosted a party outside the store, with café lights strung across the parking lot, cornhole featuring beanbags made from our textiles, and a floral-arranging station with vases from the shop as a gift for guests to take home. Customers from all over the country tagged me in their photos under our sign in front of the Dutch door, holding their McGee & Co. shopping bags.

The shop would represent a small portion of our business on paper, but it filled a large space in our hearts. It was a physical manifestation of our love of design and our fans. The shop was filled with many of the same items we sold online, but their new surroundings connected the dots between beauty and livability. When people walked in they could see how to style our products and visualize how to incorporate them into their own homes. Customers knew they could ask questions and feel welcomed, regardless of their design knowledge.

As we stepped onto the plane to fly back to Utah, our shop was in the hands of our team, and we trusted them to carry out this vision.

Within three years of launching McGee & Co., we went from

selling products from a basement storage room to having our own warehouse and brick-and-mortar store, with combined sales of roughly $30 million a year. All without seed funding or series A, B, C, or D—we were the sole investors, putting in countless hours of pure sweat equity. This explosive growth had not come without stumbling blocks, but we had learned many valuable lessons along the way. Unyielding commitment and a team mentality gave us the fortitude to seek the good hidden within each obstacle. And the refinement process led us to create functional solutions with beautiful results.

thirteen

FIND BALANCE

| *Be deliberate with volume and proportion* |
| *to create a home with harmony.* |

Syd

One late afternoon in August 2018, I walked into our bedroom to find Shea lying on the far edge of our bed with her back toward me, curled into a ball, her hands covering her face. Through muffled tears she said, "I don't want to go right now."

The shades were open, and the harsh light formed a grid over her as if she were trapped. This was one day after she'd returned home from an install in the Ozarks and hours before her next flight to Minneapolis, after which she'd fly back and install a parade home in Utah, then leave four days later to go to New York. Shea kept a black Tumi toiletries bag on our bathroom counter for a year because there wasn't enough time between trips to unpack it. She'd open her suitcase on our bedroom floor, place her toiletries on the counter, throw one set of clothes into our hamper, and replace them with another set for the next trip.

My heart broke when I saw her on our bed that afternoon. She was stuck on a track I'd put her on years ago, and I felt responsible to help her get off of it.

Custom homes aren't built in a day or a week, or even a year. They take months of planning, revisions, and permitting before a subcontractor will step into an excavator and begin to dig a hole. And then you can count on another year or two to finish the home. When I said yes to a project, it was because we were stirred by the opportunity to build our future. But in a way, we were digging a hole of our own.

Commitments we'd made in our first few years of business were coming to fruition. And they were magnificent. From LA to New York, we were designing homes with waterfront properties and million-dollar furniture budgets for clients who cared about the details. We were blessed with abundance to be working on these projects, and Shea and I always said we'd rather be overwhelmed with work than trying to figure out where our next project was coming from. We had experienced the latter and were determined not to find ourselves in the same place again.

But there came a point when bounty in one area of life left us wanting for everything else—personally, with our children, and with each other. I told myself that we couldn't say no to opportunities for growth, yet our business was growing at the cost of our relationships.

Shea

In 2018, we kicked off our year with an offer we couldn't refuse, followed by months of back-to-back installs out of state. We'd received an email from Food Network with a cryptic message about an exciting opportunity. It felt like a prank, but we set up a call, hoping the email was legitimate.

Turned out they were launching their first Fantasy Kitchen giveaway, and they wanted me to design the kitchen and host the television promos with *Chopped* judge Scott Conant. The idea was that we'd design a high-end kitchen however we imagined, and they'd build it in a production studio to film all the segments. Once the sweepstakes began, viewers would enter for a chance to win $250,000 toward their dream kitchen. Their timeframe was tight, and they needed the kitchen designed within a few weeks, to give their set crew a month to bring it to life.

I wanted the kitchen to strike a delicate balance of upscale yet inviting. This kitchen would have everything. Drawing on a few elements of our modern mountain home kitchen, I wanted our work to be recognizable for viewers and hoped the high-contrast palette would pop on camera.

The set floor was a twenty-five-foot square, with light wood herringbone floors as the foundation. The kitchen would be a long U shape, with a ten-foot island in the center. The double oven range was placed under a custom stainless steel hood surrounded by white subway tile with dark grout. We installed a pizza oven, nestled in painted white brick, next to the refrigerator and a built-in homework desk.

On the opposite side of the kitchen, we designed a faux black window with sconces above and a sink centered underneath. We placed trees outside the window to give the appearance of a scenic view. The lower cabinets were painted black and the uppers were white, all with brass hardware. The island featured two different countertop materials: honed quartz with broad, sweeping gray veins and a two-hundred-pound oak butcher block on one end. The crew wheeled in the butcher block on a cart, and instead of transferring the block to the island, they built the entire island around the cart for stabilization. The butcher block was my favorite detail in the kitchen because it made a statement, but I also imagined a home cook loving the ability to chop veggies right on the island without having to grab a cutting board.

To tie in with the island's details, we designed custom steel and wood open shelving, backed by tongue-and-groove, on either side of the kitchen sink. And the set didn't end at the kitchen. We also created a warm gray butler's pantry, with plaid cement flooring that tied the kitchen and pantry colors together. The space featured two wine refrigerators, an espresso machine, and a rolling ladder to reach the tallest shelves.

We could manage the project remotely, but I was committed to several in-person visits to install the accessories and shoot the TV promos.

The first time I opened the studio door, I was awestruck. An entire kitchen floated in the middle of a warehouse, the set lights were hot, and thirty people waited for me to arrange stacked plates and a bowl of lemons. We had shipped several boxes of McGee & Co. accessories, and the production assistants had unpacked all the items and placed them on tables, ready for my arrival. I had a quick timeframe to style because I had to go to hair and makeup before the shoot.

I placed a crock of wooden spoons by the range, layered cutting boards against the backsplash, filled bottles with olive oil and vinegar next to a salt cellar, incorporated potted herbs by the sink, and finished off the island with a tall jar of silver dollar eucalyptus. When the styling was done, I stood back to admire my work and take a few photos, but was ushered over to hair and makeup to stay on schedule.

Scott and I repeated, "Enter for a chance to win," about two hundred times that day as they choreographed a routine for us: display the dishwasher, open the oven, and show off the touchless faucet. Finally, the crew said, "That's a wrap."

Instead of spending the night to enjoy some time in Manhattan, I took an Uber straight from the set to the airport so I could arrive home by the time the girls woke up the next morning.

That was my pattern: I'd awaken to them crawling on our bed in their jammies and, with rumpled hair, asking if I'd brought home a surprise. At the beginning of the year, the markers and T-shirts and sour candies were a novelty. I'd open my suitcase, see their faces light up, and feel like I was managing the juggle with grace.

Until I didn't.

A few months into weekly and sometimes biweekly trips, the jet lag went from lasting a few days to never going away. The girls were increasingly less interested in surprises and more concerned about whether I would be at school pickup or tumbling practice. My answer was, "No, I'm so sorry, sweetheart. I wish I could be there," more often than yes. I'd kiss them as they ran out the door for school, put my black toiletries bag back in my suitcase, and start the same install routine all over again.

Install day, as we call it, is the moment all of the preparation and planning come together to transform a house into a home. When the projects are large-scale, install day turns into install week. With each home we design, when the lights are hung and the paper covering the hardwood floors is pulled back, it's time for our team to get to work.

I fly to the home, with the lead designer on the project and several junior team members, to set every piece of furniture and decor into place. Prior to our arrival, everything is shipped directly to a warehouse near the house, and the movers meet us on-site to unload as we direct them. We all hold our breath, hoping the furniture will fit exactly as we intended and that issues are minimal. Something always goes awry; it's just a matter of when and what—a nick on the dresser, a vendor that shipped the wrong color rug, a lampshade that was dented in transit.

We eat lunch while standing, place fresh flowers in vases, steam the linens, and take photos and video for our portfolio. The mornings are early and we work late into the night, to leave our clients with a turnkey home. The install process usually takes more time than anticipated, and we end up sprinting through the airport to catch our flight home. As designers, it is the most stressful time and also the most gratifying.

So a year that started with a calendar full of opportunity—partnering with Food Network, a Brooklyn penthouse for *Real Simple* magazine, a top-to-bottom renovation in Calabasas, another remodel in Orange County, a Park City showcase home, several local projects, two catalog shoots, Markets in Vegas and High Point, product development trips for McGee & Co., three lake houses, and finally breaking ground on our own house—began to drain my fervor for accomplishment.

Our lofty dream of again owning a home was finally becoming a reality, but I was too distracted with other things to relish the process. This was the home we'd visualized when we left California. It was the return on our investment, a place to call our own. It was the home where we planned to take school pictures on the front porch and chart the girls' heights on the wall. But this home—our home—became one more item on the to-do list. As we checked off one install after another, I had hoped to feel a sense of achievement, but there was no time to bask or celebrate because I immediately was on to the next project.

When we entered August, my busiest month, I wanted to quit. I wanted to crawl into the hole we'd dug for ourselves and have a good, long ugly cry. Also, I wasn't working out, and I had sinus infections every few weeks, adrenal fatigue, thyroid problems, and an aching heart. I'd tell myself that I'd feel better after this trip or when we finally completed that install, but that never happened.

So the day Syd found me in a fetal position on our bed, I had lain down to let the sun wash over me and feel what I hadn't let myself feel in months. I was weary and heartbroken, but also afraid of change. Not the changes themselves, but how they would impact our lives. I loved my family *and* my career. I questioned if it was possible to have both. Did something always have to give?

I was worried that if I overcorrected, the pendulum would swing too far in the opposite direction and we'd lose momentum and, therefore, our livelihood. I wasn't sure how to handle the response that followed a no. The truth, I realized, was that my actions were saying yes to work and no to relationships. But no amount of opportunity or accomplishment could make up for missing my children, my husband, and myself.

Syd

While Shea was traveling, the girls and I would get into a routine, but a piece of us was always missing. I could never put their bows in quite right, and the servers knew our order at In-N-Out. I did my best to hold down the fort at the office, holding daily check-ins with each team and solving problems so Shea didn't have to worry while she was gone.

After she survived the month of August with Las Vegas Market, an install in the Ozarks, another in northern Minnesota, the Park City showcase home, and our McGee & Co. winter catalog shoot, we were scheduled to take a trip to New York together. Our e-commerce business was in its second year, and we were going to meet with manufacturers to finalize an entire year's worth of exclusive product developments. Our meetings were sporadic, which left us time to shop, eat, and stroll through one of our favorite cities, just the two of us.

When I go to New York, I arrange my schedule around food and a walk between each meal, alternating between cupcakes, pizza, and pizza. Our last meeting of the day was on the Upper East Side, so we rode bikes through Central Park over to the West Side for dinner at Jacob's Pickles. I always order the biscuits and gravy, while Shea scours the menu for a salad.

As I sat in the narrow restaurant across from Shea, who was wearing red lipstick and a clip in her hair, it occurred to me that we might actually be on a date.

"Is this a date?" I asked, and she laughed.

"You don't even recognize a date when you see one."

The truth was that I couldn't remember the last time we'd gone to dinner that didn't involve a work event. The lines between work and life had blurred so drastically that we counted our time in the same places as time together.

While sprinting toward our dreams, we'd left our priorities behind. We were equating busyness with success, but to what end? It had been clear after our Cancún trip, and it was clear now: we needed to pull the brakes and reconnect again. Every time we said we'd take measures to slow down, the boundaries we put in place to balance work and life eventually disappeared. And as they disappeared, I watched Shea lose her joie de vivre.

"I'm worried about you," I said.

Shea

"I'm not happy," I told him. At one time I saw the tradeoffs between entrepreneurship and life outside of the office as energizing. Both roles balanced my love of creativity and family. I am a wife, a mother, and an entrepreneur. But somewhere the scales had tipped too far in one direction, and I was losing myself in the process.

"I feel like I'm treading water," I told Syd. "And as much as I flail my arms and legs, I'm barely keeping my head above water." I was exhausted and in so deep that I couldn't see a way out of the situation. I was afraid that if I said no to clients and projects and time with our team, we'd lose everything we'd sacrificed to build. However, building a relationship with my husband and children was worth more than any business.

It was time to take another risk, but this one had nothing to do with money or houses or moving.

Syd

Our phones stayed in our pockets at dinner, and we asked each other the question of why: *Why were we doing this?* What grew out of a passion had turned into a necessity, to support our family. But a few years into the business, support had taken on a new meaning. I loved working with Shea to establish a vision and mapping out a plan with each team to take us there. I was honored to be able to hire people with skill sets beyond my own and to lean on their specialized knowledge about everything from finance to fulfillment and manufacturing. I looked forward to the social aspect of working with our beloved team, doing whatever I could to provide the resources and environment for achievement.

Even so, the deeper I involved myself in day-to-day tasks rather than maintaining high-level oversight, the less energized and effective I became. Also, Shea wanted the flexibility to be home more often and to have outlets that granted her the freedom to create homes, vignettes, marketing content, and products. As McGee & Co. grew, she'd fallen in love with the product development side of our business and wanted more time to focus her attention there. That endeavor blended all of her passions because she could design products, incorporate them into our home designs, and then develop marketing content.

At the core, we still shared our earliest vision for the brand, but we now had a team of talented minds to help us achieve that vision. We'd set out to create a brand that shared the message that beautiful design could feel approachable, and we had a thousand different ways to accomplish that mission. Shea's pace wasn't sustainable, and to help her, I was resolute in my decision to make significant changes to our business, now.

I started sending emails from the plane. "Turn off the new project form on the website," I typed. "We have enough work to get through six months, and we need the time to reevaluate the business." Inquiring homeowners were outraged when they saw the message on our website that our roster was full and to reach out again the following year. In the past I would've started making exceptions, but I wouldn't make that mistake again.

I took notes from Shea and interviewed the design team about what made the process more enjoyable for everyone involved. We raised our rates, cut our workload in half, restricted locations to nearby states, and decided to only take projects with clients we were genuinely excited to work with. Lastly, we weren't going to commit Shea to an appearance at every install. She'd attend the ones that worked within her new schedule and let our capable teams run the ones that didn't. I was dogged about bringing back balance to the force and giving Shea a moment to catch her breath. I couldn't make up for lost time, but I could reshape what was next.

Shea

As the year came to a close and Syd implemented sweeping changes to our design business, I underwent sinus surgery and was required to take the entire month of December off to recover. I can't believe I'm saying this, but the gauze stuffed up my nose and a migraine for days was one of the best things to ever happen to me because I was forced to stop. Not just slow down, but slam on the brakes, tires screeching—full stop.

I wore stretch pants for weeks, the girls beat me over and over at their favorite memory game with princesses on the cards, and I let them sneak too much dough while making chocolate chip cookies with sea salt sprinkled on top. I was there when they woke up and there when they went to sleep.

Somewhere in between, I started going for walks by myself. It was the first time in a year I had a moment to clear my stuffy head and begin to push the pieces of my life into a space that felt right.

When designing a room, I like to strategically place large pieces throughout the space and use different proportions of furniture, so a room doesn't feel flat. Instead of buying a furniture set, I'll put one large sofa with a skirted base across from two lounge chairs on delicate legs, with a rustic coffee table in the center. I'll place a small ceramic accent table between the chairs and a tall floor lamp in the corner, so the silhouettes are varied while maintaining balance in the room as a whole. I had been pushing all of my furniture up against the wall, and I needed to redistribute the pieces to feel peace and balance in my home again.

On my walks I thought about the things that excited me. I loved my time at home with our family, and I loved having time to immerse myself in the creative direction of projects and products. I loved working with our marketing and visual merchandising teams on photoshoots and videos. I enjoyed travel that invigorated my senses rather than drained them. I enjoyed squeezing in an hour of exercise, and I wanted to make time to date Syd again.

One night during my recovery, we hired a sitter and Syd and I went on a real date. Well, sort of. All I could handle was a trip to Chick-fil-A. But there were no kids or coworkers, so it was a date. I didn't ask about work, which made for a quiet ride to the drive-through.

We started talking about bucket lists, places we wanted to see, and life in our one-day house. Once the conversation was rolling, we didn't want it to stop. It felt good to laugh and tease and dream together again.

We were starting to move all the pieces from one side of our lives and balance them throughout. I started paying more attention to spacing, but this time it was for our family, not furniture. I scaled back travel, left my phone in another room when with my family, and trusted our team to actualize the vision. I had arrived at an inflection point and made the choice to live each minute with more intention.

In design, you can find balance without symmetry. My quest to live a more deliberate life wasn't about dividing my time equally across all categories. I needed to step back and look at life as a whole. Some days or weeks would be filled with picnics and jumping on the trampoline, and others would be surrounded by tile samples. This new dance required constant vigilance so I could sway back and forth between all the things that mattered most and not be swept away. By scaling back, I was giving myself the opportunity to live more abundantly.

fourteen

OPEN DOORS

*The most beautiful rooms are the ones
you enjoy with the people you love.*

Syd

We were making changes. Real, tangible changes, in our lives, our work, and our relationships. After years of sacrifices and pouring everything we had back into the business, we were beginning to pause long enough to enjoy the fruits of our labor.

Every day we drove by our lot to see the progress happening at the house. Our house, *the* house, was finally underway. When we left our California home to start Studio McGee, we spent years designing for others. Building a custom home for ourselves felt like wishful thinking and a far-off ideal. But now the foundation was poured, the framing was in progress, and Shea was in her element.

We'd pull up and Shea would jump out of the car and do a lap around the house while the girls did laps of their own on scooters in the cul-de-sac. She'd meet with our contractor, answer questions, and double-check that the designs were being implemented as specified. Before long Shea would poke her head out of the arched front door and yell, "Will you come in for a second? I need your opinion on a few things."

I'm happy to give my opinion, but if she decides to go in the opposite direction, it's best for both of us if I roll with it. In the early days of our business, our relationship became contentious when we stepped on toes and became defensive. But Shea and I have discovered that a critical component to maintaining a healthy relationship as a couple and as business partners is the ability to stay in our own lanes while reaching across the dotted line to hold each other's hand. Shea doesn't criticize me when I restructure our org charts, and I don't tell her how to design houses. Our partnership is built on unyielding trust and support, so at the end of the day we can walk through the door with open arms for each other.

I may not be a designer, but I can help her keep a level head when she starts to fixate on every little nuance. I'd laugh when she'd ask me about countertops that differed by fractions of an inch. "The details matter!" she'd say. I also can read her well enough to know when she has a favorite option but needs me to provide confirmation. "All of these white paint colors are exactly the same," I'd tease her. But I could see in her face which one she wanted me to pick.

With our own home she was feeling the pressure of anticipation—this house was a culmination of everything we had worked and sacrificed for. We're a team, and when the pressure is on, sometimes you just need to squeeze your partner's hand. "It's going to be great," I said. "Can you even believe this view?"

It may have taken years for the right circumstances to build our home, but when the time came, we knew it was right because it felt easy. Over the years we've grown more accustomed to trusting that time will show us the way. If we're putting forth an honest effort, the pieces of our lives will fall into place as they were intended. We'll push and push and push, fighting to make something happen, only to make one connection or call or misstep that allows a new door to swing wide open.

Then we look back and see that both the good and the bad, it was all meant to be.

Shea

When we were in our Pierpont office, I met with a potential client who was my same age and had two children who were within a few years of our girls. Her husband was a developer, and they were planning to build a custom home for their family. They had their lot and the plans, and we hit it off immediately. We had a similar style and taste, and our husbands both loved to ride bikes. We spent a year designing the house, but then they decided to sell their lot and hold off on building because the neighborhood wasn't a good fit.

We heard from them a few years later because they were ready to design their dream home again. This time his company was purchasing a property to be developed into a cul-de-sac of custom homes, with sweeping views of the Rocky Mountains. During one of our design meetings, I mentioned that we happened to be looking at lots to build our own home. "We could be neighbors!" they said. "You should at least go check out the area." That evening, Syd and I piled the kids into his truck and drove over to the land. The road ended in a field and we went off-roading until we arrived at the back of the future cul-de-sac. Schools and parks were within walking distance, and best of all, we'd have friends nearby and neighbors who liked us. We didn't need to look at other listings or talk to real estate agents. This was it—the place we would raise our family.

That night I started drawing plans for the house. The exterior materials would be a combination of painted white brick, siding, and stone reminiscent of an old cottage. I'd been collecting hundreds of images on secret Pinterest boards and loved the classics with a modern twist: cedar shingles, large white windows with tons of natural light, a glossy black front door, a trellis above the garage, and hydrangeas—lots of hydrangeas. There would be a bluestone porch with potted boxwoods and a backyard with a fence. Our rental homes never had fences, and it scared me to let the girls play in the backyard without watching their every move. We'd have a playhouse, a built-in barbecue setup for Syd, and a kitchen with a French Lacanche range for me.

Our daily life looked a lot different now than when I'd designed our first home. We had two young children, I actually enjoyed cooking, and this home was more than a portfolio builder. Instead of visualizing the growth of our business from the finished result, I imagined the people we'd share this home with. I wanted to open the large bifold doors across the back of our house and see family and friends chatting inside and out while the kids cartwheeled in the grass.

The kitchen would be the heart of the home and the first room I designed. It would set the tone for every other space I designed in the house. I envisioned a thirteen-foot island with Calacatta marble countertops and two-tone cabinetry. We wanted to stain the island dark brown and paint the perimeter cabinets cream, with a plaster hood above the white French range that took six months to arrive via ship. We finished the kitchen with olive-green leather pendants above the island and unlacquered brass fixtures and latches. I wanted the brass to patina over time, aging gracefully as we opened every cabinet and filled each pot of water.

Syd and I loved old homes, but we also enjoyed the function-ality of new ones. We wanted the house to have a modern classic aesthetic and also conform to our lifestyle as a rambunctious young family. All Syd cared about was the half-pipe in the basement. Yes, a half-pipe. When we left California, we both missed the ocean, but the move was especially hard on Syd. He vowed that whenever we built a house, we'd dig a pool-sized pit for an in-ground ramp, and I agreed. His win was also a win for me because he was very agreeable with all my other selections in the home.

I had a running list of features I loved from client projects and a list of all the things that bothered me about our rentals. I enjoyed homes that mixed open concept and closed spaces, vaulted ceil-ings, and wood beams. I wanted storage for everything, so the puzzles didn't fall on my head when I opened the coat closet. My number one request to our architect was "Give me all the natural light." I wanted windows everywhere so I could feel the sunshine even in the coldest days of winter.

Creating a floor plan that flowed smoothly from one room to the next, while also fulfilling our family's needs, was straight-forward. But once the framing started and I needed to begin ordering the finish materials, I became my own worst client.

I had this picture in my mind of tumbled limestone on the exterior of our home, which would cover our chimney and wrap across the back elevation of the house. There would be a large expanse of white doors, with traditional grids that folded open, to join our living room and covered patios together. I owe those stonemasons a handwritten apology, because it took me not one, two, or even three samples to get the right combination of color, grout, and texture. It took me eight different mockups, and the side of our home became a stone showroom for the whole town.

I wanted everything just right for our family. A home is a legacy, and I had the honor of designing a space to create memories for our family and other families long after we're gone.

In the midst of all the design and construction, we also were documenting every step of the process beyond our usual home tours. Typically, we shot projects when they were completed but didn't show an in-depth look behind the scenes. Between location restraints and wanting to respect our clients' privacy, we didn't capture the changes and indecisiveness during the process. But with our own home, we had the freedom to share our experiences along the way.

Syd

When we started building, we moved from our grumpy Salt Lake City neighborhood to a short-term rental a few blocks away from our new home. Remember the fateful August of 2018, when Shea was overextended with work and client installs? I failed to mention that we also had chosen to move that month. That way we could check on the house on the way to work, on the way home, on the weekends, and sometimes during lunch. Around the time we were beginning to drywall and the home was starting to take shape, we received a call that Netflix wanted us to fly out to LA for a meeting. The details were vague, but they were interested in what we were doing and wanted to hear more.

We had sworn off TV, but Netflix was different. They didn't play by traditional television rules and we were fans of their brand. If an outlet was aligned with our audience and would be open to us having an alternative format, it was going to be them. We said yes to a meeting and were excited to hear what they had in mind.

I planned to trim my beard, show up on time, and be myself. Shea, however, doesn't know how to go into a meeting empty-handed.

"What if they ask us about show concepts?" she said.

"Well, let's brainstorm a few ideas to be ready if they ask," I told her.

That sent her into planner mode, and she began meeting with our marketing team to prepare a packet filled with five show ideas that centered around our business. Once the presentation was printed, she said, "What if this isn't enough? Don't you think we should have a sizzle reel prepared, just in case?" I agreed. This time we weren't going to let someone pitch their version of us. We were going to be ourselves.

When we walked in and sat down, their acquisitions team cut straight to the chase: "If you did a show, what would it look like?" I was relieved Shea had overprepared for the meeting. She reached into her bag and pulled out her laptop and copies of our presentation. We shared our concepts and the sixty-second sizzle reel about us, our family, our work family, and our passion for designing homes.

After a few trips back and forth, finalizing the deal, partnering with a production company, and agreeing on a show format, we were rolling. Our first day of filming was one month before we were planning to move into our new home.

We had a firm moving date because the owner had sold the rental home we were living in. Regardless of whether our home was finished, we'd be moving into either the garage or a Residence Inn for a few weeks. Our contractor, Tyler, knew it was a tight deadline and worked around the clock to finish. The cabinets were going in, the painters were in every room, and the electricians lived on ladders. I could tell we'd be cutting it close.

I didn't sleep well the night before our first day on camera, so I drank two sugar-free Red Bulls and a Monster Energy on the way to the site. Not only was I shaking from the caffeine, but I couldn't decide if I was going to throw up or crap my pants or both at the same time.

We kept waiting for the moment they'd tell us to stop being us and start playing a character. But they never did, and we both started to relax. Somehow I managed to maintain control of my bodily functions, tell a few jokes, and not make a complete fool of myself on camera.

Shea

The first day of filming I woke up with the largest zit of my life. No amount of professional makeup application could hide my entire cheek. But we couldn't back out now. I was nervous too, but instead of Red Bull I had a forty-four-ounce Diet Coke hidden in my tote bag. The producers gave us a few design beats to cover, but we were shocked at how little they said to us. They told us over and over that they wanted Syd and me to be genuine and didn't overly direct us. Almost to the point where Syd and I would ask, "Are you sure you want us to talk about this? We have no idea what we're doing."

I was elated to see they also were taking great care to format the show to capture our design vision. The crew followed us to breakfast, site visits, the office, on shopping trips, and even documented our moving day. We were mixing high-end estates with smaller one-room projects, to share a diversity of homes, and they were shooting in our signature light-filled style. The producers were capturing us in an authentic way and shared our belief that good design could happen whether your budget was $2 million or $20,000.

Our home passed inspection, but it wasn't completely finished, so we decided to move the whole family into my studio above the garage. I had picked this gorgeous wool carpet to go in the upstairs bedrooms, but it was back-ordered. I believed it was worth the wait. There was plywood on the floors where the carpet was supposed to go and dust everywhere, but we were moving into our home!

The day we started our business, we'd visualized what this day would look like. I'd imagined shutting the doors of a well-organized van, pulling up to a manicured lawn, turning the handle of our new front door, and walking into a move-in-ready home. That vision wasn't going to be a reality. And while we were excited, anxiety bubbled as we tried to figure out the whole "act natural for the camera" thing.

The movers were in our rental house along with the production crew, who followed us with cameras, lights, and sound equipment as we scrambled to gather the last few stray items. Our boxes were in the truck, and the plunger I'd forgotten to pack was in the back of my car with our suitcases for the next few weeks, but we still needed to disconnect the washer and dryer.

Syd was in the laundry room, and I heard him swearing.

"What is that smell?" I yelled.

"Just a little gas leak," Syd mumbled. "It's fine. It's fine."

The camera guys weren't going to miss the action, so they pulled their T-shirts over their noses and kept filming. I tried to remain calm, avoid the cameras, and usher the girls out to the car. Syd got the leak under control, and we all caravanned to the new house. We pulled onto our street and couldn't find a parking spot because construction crews were everywhere, trying to finish the house. We unloaded our belongings in the garage and laid two mattresses on the floor of my studio.

The first nights in our home were spent on the floor, the door shut to block out paint fumes, with shoes next to our beds in case we needed to go to the bathroom and had to walk across the plywood floor. As inconvenient as the situation was, this is my favorite memory in the house. The girls looked forward to our slumber parties every night, and we were all excited to be together under our new roof.

Before we unpacked the boxes in our garage, we needed to shoot our McGee & Co. winter catalog. It was ninety degrees outside and we hadn't even put any underwear in our dressers, but the team was there, setting up a Christmas tree. Tawnee, our VP of marketing, and Kristine, our VP of visual merchandising, have been by my side since the early days of our business. We speak the same design language and are protective of maintaining the standards we have built together for the brand.

Kristine had a checklist for the visual team to create ornament flat lays for shooting product with a bird's-eye view on our herringbone wood floors, hang cable-knit stockings by the fire, and tie velvet ribbons on the tree. Tawnee directed the videographer and photographer on what angles needed to be captured and told Syd and me to look like we loved each other. I wore heels and holiday attire to pose for the catalog, while analyzing the vignettes and making adjustments. "Let's move the branches to the left and pull the artichokes two inches forward," I'd say.

It was chaotic to move in, style our home, and decorate for Christmas all while on camera. But the activity wasn't stressful to me. I was doing what I loved with people I loved. This was home.

As we settled in over the next few months, I never wanted to leave the house. Every corner was how I had dreamed it would be and was a collection of experiences and lessons learned. The vintage basket under our kitchen island was from the time Syd and I had run through the rain, with the basket over our heads, at the Rose Bowl Flea Market, and the marble cutting board in our pantry was a remnant from our countertops in California. The curved sofa in our living room was one of our first exclusive furniture designs, and the picture on Syd's desk was from the time he had taken the girls surfing at Doheny State Beach.

Syd

Something I don't tell Shea nearly often enough is how much I love walking into a space she has designed. My cheesiness is about to top the charts, but it feels like magic to me. She has the ability to create a calming environment that is both inspiring and comfortable. My favorite spot in the house is the vantage point from the kitchen sink, where I can see into the living room and dining nook, as well as out to the playhouse in the backyard.

At first it was like living in one of our catalogs. It was hard to believe I was standing in the elusive house we'd talked about on our Sunday drives.

A month after we moved in, the carpet was installed, and construction was nearing completion on the main floors. As we settled and made a few messes, the house felt more like home. To finish construction faster and streamline our filming schedule, we opted to leave the basement unfinished and, therefore, my beloved half-pipe too. We also built an interview set in our basement to eliminate the back-and-forth to a studio.

When you walk downstairs, there's a twenty-foot-wide temporary wall with a fake living room, camera equipment, and lights. My favorite joke is to tell people, "Mommy and Daddy are filming a movie in the basement."

Building the interview set in the basement directly aligned with the changes we were continuing to make in our business and life. Shea would get ready in the morning at the kitchen island while I made pancakes with the girls, and then they'd ask Shea for a little blush before heading off to school.

Shea

When I listed the things about my job that pulled me out of bed in the morning—designing, directing visuals, and creating content—I didn't anticipate doing a TV show. However, it was a natural addition to our webisodes, which we still enjoyed putting up on social media.

I've always loved creating spaces for people, knowing that good design can improve their lives. Hearing clients share their personal experiences during filming has confirmed that belief. They have opened up about trials, shared stories of loss, and expressed how our work brought them hope and beauty. Design impacts our mood and the way we feel. We tend to spend more time with the people we love in spaces created with intention.

When I planned our home, I considered how to make our use of the spaces flow smoothly and feel pretty—everything from making dinner to taking a shower, even the way I'd hang the garland on our banister during the holidays. I imagined the girls in their red-stripe pajamas, running down the stairs past swags of cedar.

After setting up our Christmas tree again a few months after our catalog shoot, we hosted our annual pie night as a family. Instead of dessert as an afterthought on Thanksgiving, we make it a whole event the night before. Everyone comes with an empty stomach and a pie, and we indulge in the food and the company.

Syd's parents flew up from California, and my parents, my brother's family, cousins, aunts, and uncles all joined us in our home. The fire was lit, Frank Sinatra played in the background, and we lined up over a dozen pies and charcuterie spreads across our kitchen island. There was pecan pie, peach pie, coconut pie, and chess pie, and meats and cheeses arranged like art on reclaimed bread boards. For Syd and me, food coupled with design is the way to the heart. We were proud of our new surroundings, but mostly excited to use them as a gathering place.

A home is an opportunity to invite people in, share warmth, and spend time together. The night was full of love and crumbs as we told stories and tested every slice of pie. Syd and I had opened the door and were beginning to embrace life. It was messy, it was beautiful, and we were happy.

fifteen

ELEVATE THE EVERYDAY

| *Don't stop creating.* |

Shea

One day when we were sitting in our Pierpont office with space heaters at our feet and a charred ceiling above us, I wondered aloud how long it would take to feel like we'd made it. Syd's response was, "They say it takes five years for a business to hit its stride—and then we'll just be getting warmed up." I didn't want to hear what he had to say, so I put my head down and kept creating.

"What does 'making it' look like, anyway?" he'd asked. I didn't have an answer to his question. I wanted to believe that running a business was like climbing a mountain, and at some point, after grinding away, we'd reach what I perceived to be the top. When things were difficult, the planner in me wanted to put a deadline on our business so we could check the success box, and then life would be easy. At the precipice of our entrepreneurial journey, I equated success with a life devoid of struggle.

I imagined there would come a time when we had solutions to every problem and could anticipate issues before they appeared.

My perspective has evolved during our journey, and I've discovered that entrepreneurship more closely resembles a long expanse of rolling hills heading into the horizon. From chasing a dream to facing the realities that followed, we have spent years learning about ourselves and each other, leading a team, and making tough calls. There were plenty of problems, but there were even more victories. When we were denied a loan to purchase a small fixer-upper, we felt defeated. It would have been the first step in promoting our business. The plan failed, but we pivoted and kept going. When we attended Market for the first time and vendors turned up their noses at us, we were crushed. Now, when I see our warehouse filled with products being shipped to our customers, I'm more grateful than if it had been handed to us on a Delft blue platter.

As we grew as a design firm, our projects also grew in budget, size, and scope. Our team was handed the reins to try new ideas, break the rules, and push our creative limits. But we didn't start there. We began with clients who often viewed us as an ordering service and worked for years to develop our brand into a trusted resource. I started with a set of bookshelves and have since designed everything from mountain retreats to beach houses, farmhouses, lake houses, pool houses, and main houses. I have wallpapered ceilings in million-dollar kitchens and said prayers that a custom sectional would make it up the stairs. I have also worked with hand-me-down furniture and used rocks as bookends to save money.

No two projects have ever looked alike, and I have learned with each of them. I don't want the learning that comes from creating to stop. So I won't stop creating. With each estate, room, photo shoot, or vignette, the principles of good design transcend their breadth. The same rules of proportion, balance, juxtaposition, and texture work in all contexts.

The principles we apply on a large scale can be distilled down to narrow vignettes and applied in any home. When designing a large-scale project, like a kitchen, we begin by visualizing the outcome and consider the layout and overall aesthetic. We ask the homeowner about functionality and storage needs. We draw the elevations, starting with a clean slate, and add layers as we go. Are the cabinets the right height for the ceiling? Do the light fixtures fill the space above the island? Once construction begins, the process is messy and we have a few hiccups along the way. But after the kitchen is installed, we fill empty countertops with accessories, to bring character and interest to the space.

When designing an entry vignette, the scope of the design is smaller, but we also begin by imagining what it can become. We develop a focal point, typically a console with a mirror or artwork above, and ensure the size adequately fills the wall space. We'll look at functionality and add baskets for stray shoes or layer an ottoman to sit on. After the main pieces are in place, we'll add a lamp and accessories: stacked books, a vase, and a bowl for keys. Once the design is implemented, we take a step back, adjust as needed, and feel a little brighter every time we walk by our creation.

We reached our five-year anniversary as a business a few weeks before moving into our new home. When I pull into our driveway after a long day at the studio, I smile because I know what it took to get us here. I enter through the garage and drop my bag on the counter, thankful to share this joy with my husband and children.

One of the hardest and most rewarding aspects of running a business as a husband-wife team is that we often experience the highs and lows in unison. When we're feeling the weight at work, we both feel it. But when we're sitting at our dinner table, with the golden hour streaming through our windows, listening to the girls' chitchat, our eyes will meet in mutual appreciation for the life we've built together. Learning to push through challenges has awarded us the wisdom to relish the good moments. And relishing good moments has propelled us to push through the challenges.

We are now garnering recognition for our work and beginning to enjoy the return on our investment. In a way, it does feel as though we are hitting our stride. We're certainly miles ahead of the lost young couple who decided to sell their home in hopes they could start a business. Our love has been tested, but Syd and I gained a deeper understanding of what it meant to be partners in life and business. We have learned to set boundaries, even if they are imperfect at times, to balance our roles as entrepreneurs and parents.

As Syd said, I believe we are just warming up. What is "making it," anyway? We can set goals and reach them, but life will never hand us a perfect set of circumstances to get where we want to go. I've realized that the problems change, but there are always problems. Our success lies in taking the next step.

We're not sharing our story with you because we've made it; we're sharing our story with you because we're in the middle of it. The new possibilities ahead are only possible because of what is behind us. As we embark on new opportunities, we still want to honor our roots.

When we moved into our first rental home in Salt Lake City, I discovered that one of the few perks of the neighborhood was the proximity to a Super Target. It was eleven minutes from our garage to the parking lot. Wren was my shopping buddy, and I'd buckle her into the front seat of the red cart and roam the store. We'd start in the grocery department and work our way to the diapers and then over to the home section. Syd and I had just sold everything to start our business and needed to stretch our savings as far as they could go. I would work my way down each aisle, looking at the bedding, organizational items, and shelves filled with decor. Displays featured designers I admired, like Nate Berkus, and I'd think to myself how wonderful it would be to see my name on those signs one day.

It brought me great joy to tack a ten-dollar basket or vase onto our grocery bill without feeling like I was putting us in grave financial danger. Sometimes I bought a new candle or a pot, and other times I purchased a tray, picture frame, or doormat. These decorative items were by no means essential, but they were small pick-me-ups during a rocky time for our family.

As soon as the groceries were put away, I'd light my fresh candle or fill a new vase with water and clip lilac branches from the tree in our yard. Adding touches of beauty to our ordinary surroundings lifted my spirits and inspired me to continue creating. It buoyed me to walk past the updated arrangement on my kitchen counter or the greenery on our table. These subtle touches made a tremendous difference in our home, even if it wasn't magazine-worthy.

Don't wait. Your home may not have the shiny new backsplash or the French oak floors you always wanted, but don't let that hinder you from composing pretty moments in your home that excite you and bring people together. Design is about creating and looking for opportunities to elevate the everyday. The art of making changes to your surroundings can brighten your perspective and starts with seeing the potential. Whether the motion is as simple as buying a new pillow or as large as knocking out a wall, the transformative power of design has moved me, and I never want to stop creating. My hope would be for you to do the same.

When I suggested to a business associate that my dream was to work with Target just as much as it was to design high-end homes, he raised his eyebrow, shocked that partnering with a value-driven brand was a goal. He asked me to explain my reasoning, and I told him, "Because there was a time when a ten-dollar vase had the power to change my day."

As a designer, I appreciate the technique of hand-knotted rugs, the wrinkles of imported Belgian linen, and pottery thrown on a wheel instead of made by a machine. My eye has always been drawn to fine details, and I admire the artistry and craftsmanship that goes into high-end goods. But I also believe beauty can be found in the everyday, and sometimes that beauty shares the same cart as your Cheerios.

Syd

When we received word that Target leaders were interested in meeting with us at our office, even Shea had no idea what to prepare. We were both nervous and thrilled to even be on the radar of a company we admired. We had the team clear the clutter from their desks, placed flowers in the lobby from a leftover photo shoot, and lined up bottles of ice-cold Topo Chico on the conference table.

Before the meeting, Shea and I discussed what we believed we could contribute to a potential partnership. Although our business was small in comparison, we believed in ourselves, the Studio McGee vision, and that we had something to offer. We both knew our brand's modern classic style was a natural fit with Target, but we also saw an opportunity to bring more furniture to their offering. Our experience creating high-end homes and products gave us a unique perspective to deliver home furnishings in a more accessible way.

When they arrived, we shared our story, more insight into our business, and our collaborative process between designing interiors and products. Shea was jittery before the meeting, but that stopped the second she started talking about her passion for details, mixed materials, and juxtaposition in design.

It was hard for me to suppress a chuckle when they asked about Shea's knowledge of Target's different home collections. Shea was a fan and rattled off every line and collaboration from the last five years. She could list her favorite products and even the price points—she'd been doing her homework for years before this meeting. It was clear she adored the brand and its ability to deliver good design to a wide audience at an attainable price point. Just as Shea mixes high and low pieces in her designs, this partnership rounded out our offering to fans who followed us for design inspiration and were looking for a pick-me-up to brighten their day. We signed the deal and a few weeks later, Shea flew to Minneapolis to present concepts to their team.

After working on the collection for a year, it sold out online within minutes, and Shea had already begun designing for the next seasons.

Forging connections has increased our capacity to share our design perspective on a larger scale, but these partnerships with large brands like Netflix and Target have only been part of that reach. Every employee, follower, client, customer, and business partner is a connection that has shaped our business.

Our brand is known for its light and airy style, but this approach permeates more than visuals. Our marketing team creates style guides for graphic design, so we incorporate consistent font choices, colors, and layouts when developing content across all platforms. But we also have a style for the way we communicate with each other and our partners.

I always tease our team by saying that exclamation marks are very on-brand. When answering paint color questions on social media, responding with, "The color is Swiss Coffee!" is more effective than, "The color is Swiss Coffee." The use of that punctuation mark has helped us build a community of millions of people because we show that we're grateful for them, their questions, and their input.

Every touch point is an opportunity to build a relationship. Our connections are everything, and we make it a point as a team to communicate in an uplifting and positive way. Boiling with anger and sending degrading messages don't help or change an issue. We've found that we can resolve matters just as effectively by being kind and in turn elevate the atmosphere in which we work.

Hiring smilers has been one of the best means to create an upbeat culture for our team and partners. I've interviewed hundreds of potential employees, let go of dozens, and can speak to the impact of beauty in our surroundings by creating a supportive team. Designing a business is as much about people as it is about the products and process.

When I was adrift after leaving my job and before joining Shea, I was searching for a career with meaning, something that would leave a positive mark in the world. Just like greenery in a vase, we can elevate those around us with each interaction. As the CEO of our company, you won't find me placing that greenery in a vase (Shea would end up rearranging it anyway), but I do have the opportunity to design a good environment for our team and facilitate bringing joy to people's homes and everyday lives. There will always be down times and tense situations, but we have seen these junctures turn for the better, if we handle them with care.

Shea

These downtimes have been inflection points in our business, where we were faced with a choice either to quit or to reevaluate and keep going. A trip, a surgery, a pandemic—every challenging situation has presented opportunities. We pause, mourn, and allow creativity to reinvigorate our souls.

In the middle of the worldwide COVID-19 pandemic, we were forced to permanently shut the glossy black Dutch door to our Costa Mesa store. Devastated that our shop couldn't withstand the financial implications of several months of closure, we were forced to part ways with employees we cared for and say goodbye to a shop that brought happiness to our team and customers.

Had this happened at the beginning of our journey, I wouldn't have had the ability to trust that things would eventually work out. Although we were heartbroken, we remained hopeful. Knowing the sun would follow rain didn't take away the disappointment, but it gave us the confidence to move forward. We didn't regret our decision to open a store, even though it closed unexpectedly. If we hadn't taken the leap, we would have missed the experience.

The Costa Mesa shop taught us the difference between running a brick-and-mortar and an online store, so we'll be a step ahead if we later decide to open another location. We learned that providing an in-store environment to connect with our customers was important to us, and despite this experience, we still had the desire to open a shop again in the future.

My stomach hurt while thinking about the empty shelves and how there would be no more parties on the lawn or photos under the sign. I was sad thinking of the customers who would miss walking by the vine-covered shop to grab a gift for a friend and one for themselves. Coffee in hand, they'd peruse inside while their dogs drank from the water bowl we set outside. My heart fell thinking of our customers going out of their way on beach vacations to pick up a candle to squeeze into their suitcases. This connection wouldn't be possible anymore. And I'll never forget seeing our girls twirl in the shop or holding their hands as we walked across the street to grab a doughnut. The smell of citrus and birch would soon fade, and another shop owner would fill the shelves.

But success isn't life without struggle—it's hitting your stride by embracing the adventure. Opportunity is around every corner, but we need to keep working, living, and creating, so when the time comes, we'll be ready.

This challenging season also had upsides—more hours in the day for writing, baking, playing games, and enjoying a slower life at home. We had time to learn how to watercolor and grow a garden. This was a time for family and to reevaluate our priorities, our business, and our surroundings. We were building on a foundation that was laid, but open to shifting as the tides changed within and around us.

The show, the move, the partnerships, the store, the design firm, and the office in our spare bedroom all resulted from our willingness to take risks, even when the timing wasn't perfect. At one point we had Legos in our carpet, and our business strategies rarely went according to plan, but we never stopped creating. Our journey has been messy, and we've made a lot of mistakes along the way. We've experienced challenges as a company, as a couple, and as a family, but we've been able to seek the good and turn those into opportunities.

You don't always follow your dreams in the most ideal situations. For us, there was rarely a right time to begin or a clear next step, but we faced everything head-on as we lived out our motto to *make life beautiful*.

Regardless of where you are in your journey, it's not about having all the answers—it's about seeing the potential.

ACKNOWLEDGMENTS

From our kitchen table to the studio as we now know it today, we are grateful to every employee and friend who has shared their time and talents to carry the vision forward. To our clients, who have trusted us to design the places they call home, thank you. To Carly Grimes, who paved the way with grace. To Jaimee Livingston, who set the foundation for a team with an incredible work ethic. Tawnee Walker, you have higher standards for the brand than we do ourselves. Kristine Monson, your eye is unmatched and we're thankful you now lead the team to style our bookshelves. Kelsie Lindley, we have watched you grow from intern by the swamp cooler to design leader. Roxanne Wise, you were right about switching to Shopify. Joe Jorgensen, thank you for teaching us what a pattern repeat is and supporting us even when all signs pointed to failure. Bill Stankey, thank you for seeing our potential. To every member of our team yesterday and today, thank you.

ABOUT THE AUTHORS

Syd and Shea McGee, partners in both life and business, joined forces to found their design firm, Studio McGee, in 2014, and have designed hundreds of home interiors across the country since. After graduating with a degree in communications, Shea decided to pursue her dream and pour her heart into remodeling their first home, while documenting the process. Her aesthetic captured the attention of the Instagram world, as she became one of the first design influencers on the platform. Shea's fresh approach quickly attracted a long client roster and a loyal following, motivating Syd and Shea to join forces. After their first daughter was born, the couple decided to sell their home in California and move to Utah to put everything they had into launching the business.

As their design portfolio and fan base grew, it paved the way for the launch of their e-commerce brand, McGee & Co., two years later. With the vision that beautiful design can be approachable, they have become one of the leading innovators in the interior design industry. Their firm is a premier online retail destination and continues to share their signature light-filled aesthetic with millions. Syd is the chief executive officer and founding operational leader and strategist, while Shea leads the creative direction for all visuals, marketing, and products within the Studio McGee portfolio of brands.

They live with their girls, Wren and Ivy, in the Salt Lake City, Utah, area with the Rocky Mountains as their backdrop.